ME

by HERBERT S. ZIM and SONIA BLEEKER ZIM

ILLUSTRATIONS by Virginia Bimel, Graciela Romo de Cabañas, Enid Kotchnig, William McVaugh, Eduardo Merino, George Sandstrom, Arthur Singer, Cristobal Torres and Ernesto Vasquez

flower vendor—Xochimilco

GOLDEN PRESS   **NEW YORK**

FOREWORD

This Guide to Mexico was contemplated and discussed for many years before work began. Each time it seemed more formidable to compress into a pocket guide the rich story of Mexico, its past and its present progress.

Mexico, long a tourist haven, has many guides to accommodations, services, bullfights, and attractions. This compact Guide touches on aspects of Mexico's natural history—its geography, geology, plant and animal life. It deals with the people, both native and newcomers, the archeology, history, folklore, arts, and government.

Our Guide owes much to the unstinting help of many Mexicans and North Americans. Among them are Adolfo de la Huerta, Manuel Aguilar, Oliver Austin, Ignacio Bernal, Elia Bravo, Edwin Duckles, Victor Fosado, Richard Gaines, Donald Hoffmeister, Julia Morton, Allan Phillips, Arturo Pompa, and Bernardo Villa. Our special thanks to the Departamento de Turismo and to the Instituto Nacional de Antropologia e Historia for their generous cooperation and permission to use their photographs. We are also grateful to the following photographers: K. Abert, G. Aldana, M. Boak, R. Cosentino, E. Duckles, C. Nakatani, D. Polon.

H.S.Z.
S.B.Z.

CONTENTS

Rooftops, Taxco.

VISITING MEXICO

If you join the thousands of visitors who come to Mexico to see, enjoy, and understand this land, you will receive a warm and gracious welcome. As a guest, observe the common courtesies and respect your hosts' customs. Try Spanish, even if only in greetings and polite phrases.

The visitor will find at least two Mexicos. The first, large cities and tourist resorts. These are cosmopolitan and quite sophisticated. They offer more entertainment and greater freedom in dress and behavior. The other is the Mexico of villages and rural areas, where the tempo of life is slower and more conservative—more so for women than for men. To enjoy the small markets, churches, and countryside, try a quiet, unobtrusive approach. A simple gift, such as candy for children, is more acceptable in rural areas than indiscriminate offers of coins.

Remember, as a foreigner and a stranger you are mainly on your own. Factors you may take for granted at home do not always apply here. You are subject to Mexican law. This will be important in accidents or other crises (p. 141). A stranger (especially in cities) is often a sucker and can easily become a victim. A car full of valises, clothes, and cameras is a temptation, even when locked. Do not leave automobiles in the street at night. Keep wallets and valuables safe. Be careful in crowds. Watch out for being shortchanged. If you are "taken," protest immediately and firmly. The Mexican Tourism Department now offers some legal advice and can aid you in some situations; so can the police. But the responsibility is basically yours.

HEALTH Begin with correct clothing. Mexico is cool, even cold, at night—except at low altitudes. Count on afternoon showers from mid-May through October. You will want to walk, so wear proper shoes. Some people adjust quickly to the 7,000-ft. altitude of Mexico City; others take several days. You get less oxygen with each breath, as you soon learn if you run or climb.

Mexico City and most other cities have safe drinking water. Local plumbing can be a source of contamination, however. Bottled water and soft drinks are usually available. Eat fruit that you can peel (bananas or oranges) and avoid tempting snacks in markets.

Stomach upset or diarrhea occurs. Your doctor may prescribe Enteroviaforma, Sulfasuxidina, or Neotracina—all available at larger drugstores. Mexico has good doctors, should you need one. Ask your hotel or the American Embassy for a recommendation.

MORE INFORMATION and help may be needed as you go. Before you start, get publications from the Mexican Government Tourism Department, with offices in a dozen large U.S. cities. If you are a member, use the American Automobile Association (AAA), which also has offices at five border cities. Try books from your local library and purchase one of the general tourist guides. In Mexico, the Tourism Department has a large office at Reforma, 45, and another at Av. Juarez, 89. Offices are also found in all state capitals. The Asociacion Mexicana Automovilistica (AMA) can be helpful, too.

At hotels and shops, look for the weekly guides (free), listing shops, markets, tours, and current attractions. Read the two English-language newspapers. Mexico City has one English radio station. Other stations carry English news and occasional announcements.

Market at Uruapan.

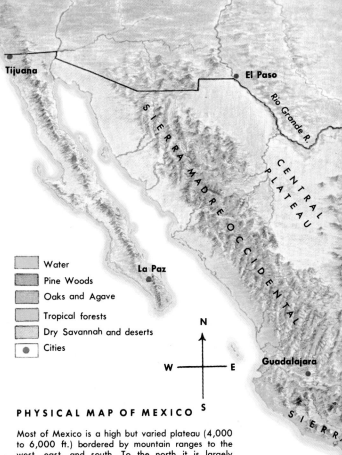

Water

Pine Woods

Oaks and Agave

Tropical forests

Dry Savannah and deserts

● **Cities**

PHYSICAL MAP OF MEXICO

Most of Mexico is a high but varied plateau (4,000 to 6,000 ft.) bordered by mountain ranges to the west, east, and south. To the north it is largely arid, broken land, with dry ranges and drier alluvial basins. To the south it merges into the Bajío, an area of rich agricultural valleys. Farther south are more mountains: first the great volcanic belt, then the Sierra Madre del Sur and the highlands of Chiapas. To the east is the wide Gulf Coastal Plain, which enlarges into the upraised platform of Yucatan.

6

THE LAND OF MEXICO

The North American continent funnels south of the Rio Grande (Rio Bravo to Mexicans) to form Mexico, where it ends in a unique kaleidoscopic country. At its widest, Mexico is about ten times the width of its Isthmus of Tehuantepec (125 miles). In length, Mexico runs about 1,800 miles. Its area is about 760,000 square miles—larger than Alaska and over twice the size of Texas.

MOUNTAINS cover much of Mexico. The great complex called Sierra Madre Occidental stretches 800 miles down the Pacific coast. Though averaging only 7,500 ft. high, the range is almost impassable. On the east is the Sierra Madre Oriental, equally long but not as high nor as complex. Between these ranges lies the high plateau that makes up over a third of Mexico. Farther south, on an east-west line, rises an imposing belt of volcanoes (p. 14) with 30 major peaks, nine of which exceed 10,000 feet. The Sierra Madre del Sur picks up south of Mexico City and pushes into the state of Oaxaca. Past the Isthmus the land rises again and the highlands of Chiapas become full-scale mountains as they pass into Guatemala.

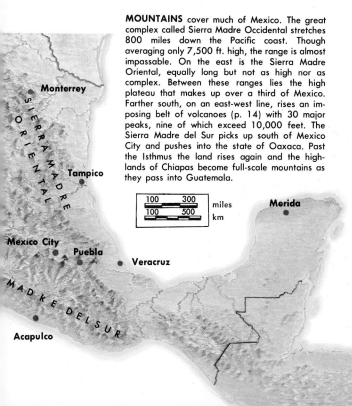

Rio Grijalva, near Frontera.

RIVERS are not a major feature in the Mexican landscape. Most are short and narrow, dropping quickly to the sea. A few are navigable near their mouths—the Rio Grande, the Coatzacoalcos, the Grijalva, and the Balsas. Other rivers have carved deep valleys as they drop from the Central Plateau, creating magnificent scenery and a water-power potential. Large dams, as on the Rio Conchos, and such waterfalls as Necaxa and Vista Hermosa, provide hydroelectric power.

SOILS along both coasts are rich, but the heavy rainfall leaches the cleared land quickly. The great volcanic belt, the basins of extinct lakes, and the larger river valleys yield crops of grain, sugarcane, fruits, and vegetables. Soils of the Central Plateau have suffered from long use, but now, with better farming practices, the yields of corn and other grains are increasing. In the north, water shortage is acute. Where irrigation is possible, cotton, beans, citrus, and other crops prosper.

Plowing with oxen.

Plowing with tractor.

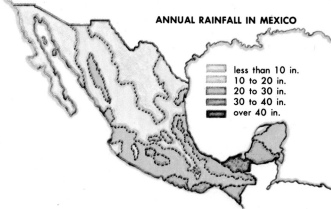

ANNUAL RAINFALL IN MEXICO

	less than 10 in.
	10 to 20 in.
	20 to 30 in.
	30 to 40 in.
	over 40 in.

CLIMATE in Mexico varies, but not as greatly as the topography suggests. A dry season (Nov.–Apr.) alternates with a rainy one (May–Oct.). Tropical areas—generally, the coasts, the Isthmus, and Yucatan—have an average temperature between 68° and 75° F., with an annual range of only about 15°. The temperate areas, mainly the plateaus and mountains that make up most of Mexico, vary from warm to cool, from moist to dry. The average temperatures here run from 50° to 68° F., with local annual ranges of about 40°—occasionally more.

CITY	Jan. Temp.	Jan. Rain	July Temp.	July Rain
Acapulco	78° F.	0.4 in.	83° F.	8.6 in.
Cuernavaca	65	0.1	68	8.6
Guadalajara	58	0.7	69	10.0
Mazatlan	67	0.5	81	6.6
Merida	73	1.2	81	5.5
Mexico, D.F.	54	0.2	61	4.9
Monterrey	58	0.8	81	2.9
Oaxaca	63	0.1	70	3.7
Puebla	54	0.2	63	5.4
San Cristobal	54	0.3	60	5.6
Taxco	66	0.0	70	12.0
Veracruz	70	0.9	81	13.8

ECOLOGICAL REGIONS are determined by a complex of factors that includes climate (especially rainfall), altitude, latitude, rocks, and soil. These set a pattern for the region's plant growth. Gradually a characteristic vegetation develops that represents the climax of local biological cycles. The development of such vegetation has a selective effect on animal life. Typical animals, especially the vertebrates, become identified with and often characterize specific habitats. Other animals are so adaptable they live in several regions.

TEMPERATE REGIONS include the northern Mexican desert (23% of Mexico)—a rugged area but one which is far from barren. Rainfall averages about 9 in. In a few places, deep-well irrigation makes agriculture possible. Plant life includes many kinds of cacti, Creosote Bush, and other shrubs. Deer and several kinds of desert quail are common. Mesquite grassland (22%) gets more rain (about 22 in. a year) and so grows a cover of grama grasses and low mesquite trees. Deer and antelope are found, with many upland birds. Unfortunately, this land is now badly overgrazed. Mesquite is being removed to encourage grasses.

Chaparral (shrubby thickets) covers only about 1% of Mexico. Rainfall is also about 20 in. on this hilly terrain of Manzanita, Chamise, and other shrubs.

The pine-oak region makes up 26% of the land. This region, with 44 in. of rainfall, supports rich forests: many oaks and about a dozen pines and junipers. Mammals, from rabbits to deer, use these woods with quail, pigeons, and songbirds. But most of the forests have been cut. The land is overgrazed and eroded. Efforts to restore the soil are under way. Finally, at the mountaintops, is a small boreal region of fir and pine, with coarse grasses and shrubs.

Tropical Mexico

The ecological regions themselves have vague boundaries. Tongues of one area often penetrate a neighboring area. Farming, grazing, and forestry constantly alter the land. A 19th-century forest zone may be desert today—without any of the original soil by which the plant cover can be restored.

Five of Mexico's ecological regions, constituting 72% of the country, are essentially temperate. The remaining 28% is frost-free, tropical terrain. But less than half of this has enough rainfall to be called "jungle."

TROPICAL REGIONS include a near-desert (cacti and all) in the arid scrub area of the Balsas Valley. Here rainfall is about 20 in. This dry region includes about 1% of Mexico. The tropical thorn forests, with a 3% area, are mainly acacias, which drop their leaves in the dry season and bloom when the rains (avg. 25 in.) begin. Tropical deciduous forests (9%) have more rain (avg. 44 in.) and more trees, which are also bare in the dry season. Wildlife is plentiful.

A region of savanna (1% of the land) runs along both tropical shores, marked by palms and palmettos, calabash trees, and low areas of coarse grasses.

The tropical evergreen forest (rainfall about 74 in.) makes up 6% of Mexico. Here the broadleaf trees—zapotes, cedars, copal, figs, and palms—are never bare. All the tropical forests are rich in wildlife—tapirs, monkeys, tinamous, macaws. The rain forest, with a distinct upper and under story, is the most typical and largest tropical region (7%), with rainfall of about 130 in., falling in the summer.

Mahogany, zapote, and other tall forest trees thrive with lianas and bamboos. Tropical mountaintops support cloud forests (1%) which, because of their altitude, include a number of temperate broadleaf trees.

11

GEOLOGY

Geologic forces acting over millions of years made Mexico's varied landscape. Almost everywhere, mountains are in sight. These and the intervening lands are formed of three kinds of rocks. Sedimentary rocks solidified from erosional debris, on land or under water. Igneous rocks are of molten origin, thrown out as lavas or cooling internally as granites. And third, the metamorphic rocks are those altered by heat and pressure.

NORTH AMERICA, squeezed down the funnel of Mexico, reveals, in a reduced space, many of the geologic features seen more widely dispersed in the north. The uplift that produced the Rocky Mountains also caused mountain building in Mexico and large-scale volcanic activity. Associated with the volcanic belt is an area of crustal strain in which earthquakes occur. This belt runs roughly from 16° to 20° N. lat. and continues, with lesser activity, up the western half of Mexico.

Much of Mexico was shallow seas during a large part of the long geologic past (p. 16), and during this period extensive deposits of limestones and shales were formed. Later, deposits of coal and oil developed in similar sediments. Limestone is common, covering much of the surface in the north and all of Yucatan. Large, beautiful limestone caves at Garcia and Cacahuamilpa are well worth seeing.

Volcanic activity, old and new (pp. 13–15), has buried large areas under lava and ash. Volcanic rocks slowly decay and make good soil. Important deposits of metals are associated with them. Newer lava flows form malpais—badlands of little economic value.

In large western areas, heat, pressure and chemical action have altered limestone to marble and produced other metamorphic rocks.

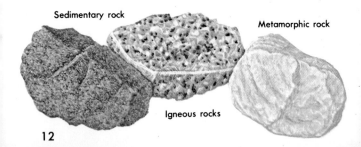

Sedimentary rock

Metamorphic rock

Igneous rocks

Volcanoes Popocateptl and Iztaccihuatl.

VOLCANOES of Mexico had their origins some 50 or 60 million years ago—about the time the Rocky Mts. were forming and volcanoes in southwestern U.S. were erupting. To this period belong Mexico's highest volcanic peaks (p. 14). Volcanic activity has continued on a lesser scale up to recent times. Xitle, on Ajusco, erupting about 2,000 years ago, produced the lava flow on which University City, D.F., is built. Jurullo, the most active Mexican volcano, still emits steam and other gases. So do Popocatepetl and Citlaltepetl. Since 1903, when the Colima volcano went off, only one volcano (Paricutin) has erupted.

REMNANTS OF VOLCANIC ACTIVITY persist long after eruptions have stopped. Final eruptions usually involve large amounts of volcanic sand and ash. As these cease, the volcano may release only steam and gases while deposits of sulfur form around the crater. When rainwater percolates down through the porous lava and is heated underground, hot springs and fumaroles form near the base of the volcano. These hot waters with dissolved minerals are said to have medicinal properties. Sometimes volcanic steam is trapped till it builds up pressure and shoots water high into the air as geysers, seen at Los Azufres and La Hoya.

EL PARICUTIN, born at 5 p.m. on Feb. 20, 1943, in an open cornfield, grew in a year to a 1,500-ft. volcano. It poured out 2 billion cubic feet of lava, destroying two villages and forcing 4,000 people to flee.

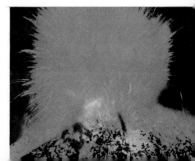

Many of Mexico's peaks rise well over 10,000 feet. The ten highest are listed below.

	Feet			Feet
1. Pico de Orizaba	18,500		6. Nevado de Colima	14,100
2. Popocatepetl	17,700		7. Cerro Zempoala	13,500
3. Iztaccihuatl	17,300		8. Cofre de Perote	13,350
4. Nevado de Toluca	14,800		9. Tacana	13,200
5. La Malinche	14,500		10. Volcan de Colima	12,900

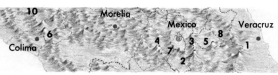

MOUNTAINS of Mexico form major ranges in the east, west, and south. Because of these and the Central Plateau, about 60% of Mexico is more than a mile high. Nearly all the mountains are volcanic. With them are extensive lava flows, without distinct craters. The largest and most imposing volcanoes form a belt across Mexico at about 19° N. lat.—roughly on a line from Veracruz through Mexico City, and Morelia to Colima. A few major volcanoes are a bit to the north, in Nayarit; two large ones are in southeastern Chiapas (Tacana and Cerro Mohinora), and the Volcan de las Tres Virgenes rises about midway in Baja California. Mountains above 13,000 feet usually have a permanent crown of snow even though they are within twenty degrees of the equator. Mountain climbing is a favorite organized sport.

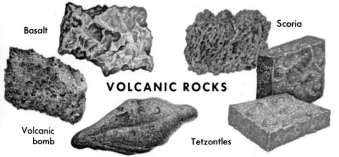

Basalt

Scoria

Volcanic bomb

VOLCANIC ROCKS

Tetzontles

BASALT, the most common lava of Mexico, forms sheets and flows, and—with scoria and ash—the large volcanic peaks. Basalt, a lava without any quartz, melts and flows easily. The Pedregal, south of Mexico City, is a fine example of a recent basalt flow. Basalt is often used in building.

RHYOLITE represents another group, the acid lavas. These contain quartz and have a higher melting point. Because of this, rhyolite lavas often come from explosive volcanoes. A number of other light lavas look similar and all are chemically like granites.

SCORIA forms when basaltic lavas are rich in gases. As lava reaches the surface, gases expand into bubbles that are trapped. Scoria may be so light it will float. Porous blocks of heavier scoria (tetzontles) are cut as a building stone. Iron in the scoria may color it a brick red.

OBSIDIAN, or Volcanic Glass, is an acid lava that has cooled very rapidly. Chemically, it resembles man-made glass. Both gradually crystallize with age. Early Mexicans developed the art of chipping and polishing obsidian to make tools, weapons, and ornaments.

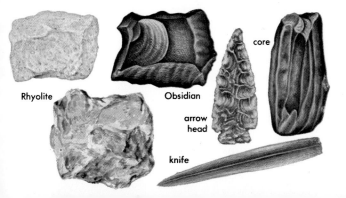

Rhyolite

core

Obsidian

arrow head

knife

MEXICO'S GEOLOGIC PAST

As the continent of North America evolved, Mexico changed with it. A glimpse of this long geologic past may help give a better picture of Mexico's land and its resources today.

Archeozoic rocks, the oldest, are ancient metamorphics, altered from still older sediments and igneous rocks. Younger granites are seen at Acapulco and elsewhere in western Mexico. During the long Paleozoic era (230–600 million years ago), shallow seas covered Mexico much of the time and thick sedimentary deposits formed. These are now on the surface in central and northern Mexico. In part of the Mesozoic era, which extended from about 63–230 million years ago, a large strait (Canal del Balsas) cut Mexico in two. Deposits of coal and oil formed in the swamps where dinosaurs and their kin lived. At the end of this period Baja California emerged, and the uplift of the Sierra Madre Oriental began.

The Cenozoic period lasted a brief 63 million years and witnessed the rise of mammals and flowering plants. Mexico had much volcanic activity and uplift continued, forming the main mountain ranges. During this mountain-building activity, rich deposits of metallic ores formed. As this period closed, Yucatan emerged from the Gulf.

Archeozoic

Paleozoic

Mesozoic

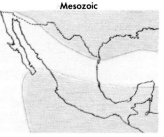

Cenozoic

PETROLEUM, the backbone of Mexico's mineral wealth (p. 148), formed during Cenozoic times in sediments that were deposited in shallow seas along the western edge of the Gulf of Mexico. Long periods of warmth stimulated the growth of untold billions of algae in the quiet waters. The oils in these tiny plants that died and were buried, century after century, are the source of petroleum. Later, earth movements concentrated the petroleum and formed oil "pools." Large amounts of natural gas accumulated with the petroleum deposits.

SINCE 1901, when the first well was drilled, Mexico has been a steady producer of petroleum. Under a regime of foreign control, production was pushed to 200 million barrels a year, making Mexico the world's second largest producer. In 1938, after expropriation, a more conservative program was initiated to protect the reserves, which amount to about 5 billion barrels. Now Mexico produces about 125 million barrels annually from some 3,000 active wells. The country is now about eighth in world production.

Mexican oil has an asphalt base, like the petroleum of California. Production comes mainly from three zones. The northern zone, around Reynosa, produces more natural gas than oil. The central zone along the Gulf coast is the major oil producer. The southern zone covers the Isthmus of Tehuantepec.

Since 1938, Pemex, the government oil company, has controlled all production and distribution. Production has increased steadily since 1945. Natural gas output-1½ million cu. ft. daily.

RECENT MEXICAN PETROLEUM PRODUCTION

Millions of Barrels

1965	133
1960	109
1955	92
1950	74
1945	44
1940	45

17

NONMETALLIC MINERALS are not a source of metals, even though some may have a metallic content, as in barite, calcite, or magnesite. Mexico has deposits that produce sufficient amounts of sulfur, fluorite, barite, graphite, dolomite, kaolin, and lime. It also has deposits of other important nonmetallic minerals, such as talc, asbestos, magnesia, and phosphates.

Sulfur

Tecali (Onyx)

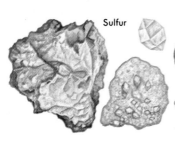

SULFUR was once gathered from around the craters of semiactive volcanoes for use in making gunpowder. Now it is obtained, in much larger amounts, from salt domes in the Isthmus. Sulfur has many chemical uses.

TECALI (Mexican Onyx) is a banded form of the mineral calcite—gray, white, rusty, greenish, or dyed in brighter colors. This soft mineral should not be confused with true onyx, a form of agate, used for ornaments.

BARITE is a heavy, fairly soft mineral of wide occurrence; colorless, white, yellow, gray, or brown. Crystals are common, often in broad plates. Barite is used in making glass, in paints and ceramics, and as a filler.

FLUORITE, a source of the active element fluorine and the gas freon, is used directly in smelting iron ores. This mineral, usually found as yellow, brown, green, or purple crystals, may occur in lead, copper, or zinc deposits.

Barite

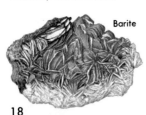

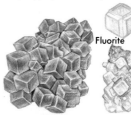

Fluorite

METALS are basic in modern technology, and Mexico has its share of them. In addition to gold and silver, which gave the country its start, Mexico has copper, zinc, lead, manganese, mercury, antimony, arsenic, tungsten, and iron. The last is now getting full industrial attention.

GOLD is widespread in Mexico and paved the way for the country's conquest. Production still continues at about 10 tons annually. Gold is found free (native gold) in stream beds, where it settles because of its weight. More is found in veins of quartz and in close association with silver, copper, and zinc. Placer gold from Chihuahua, Sonora, and Baja California is purest. That found in Guerrero and Oaxaca is alloyed with silver.

SILVER is mined at the rate of over 100 tons for each ton of gold. Mexico once produced over half the world's silver; now it produces about 17%. Some is found as native silver, but most occurs as argentite—a silvery or gray compound of silver and sulfur. Silver is also an impurity in galena (lead ore). Pure gold measures 24 carats; pure silver is 1,000 fine. Most gold is sold as 18 carats; most silver as 925 fine.

Gold Nugget

Gold Dust

Native Silver

Gold in Quartz

Argentite

Mixtec gold bells

Silver Jewelry

Mexican gold deposits

Mexican Silver deposits

THE METALLIC ORES below are minerals of importance. Most were formed as liquids and vapors from igneous rocks that penetrated limestone and other local deposits.

Galena

Sphalerite

Smithsonite

GALENA, a heavy gray compound of lead and sulfur, is the most common ore of lead. It forms large cubic crystals, often with zinc ores. Mexican galena always has some silver in it, adding to the value of the ore.

SPHALERITE, the most important ore of zinc, is a reddish-brown, resinous compound of zinc and sulfur. Exposed to moisture and air, sphalerite is altered to smithsonite, a crusty or earthy zinc carbonate mineral.

COPPER ORE is usually chalcocite —a compound with sulfur; or chalcopyrite—copper, iron, and sulfur. When moist, these primary ores alter slowly into azurite (blue) and malachite (green)—carbonates of copper with water.

TUNGSTEN, used widely in tool steel, comes from the ore scheelite (a calcium tungsten oxide) found in Sonora and Chihuahua. This light-colored mineral occurs in quartz veins or at igneous contacts with limestones.

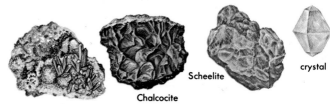

Scheelite

crystal

Chalcocite

Malachite and Azurite

Mexican deposits of Lead and Zinc

Mexican deposits of Copper

Crystals of the different minerals formed and grew in the veins and pockets. Much later, some were exposed by erosion and the deposits were discovered.

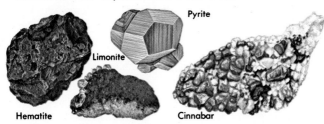

Pyrite

Limonite

Hematite

Cinnabar

IRON ORES, mainly from Durango and Baja California, are hematite and limonite, both compounds of iron and oxygen. Magnetite is a richer iron oxide found with igneous rocks. Iron pyrite (fool's gold) is an iron sulfide.

MANGANESE is used to make a tough steel alloy. Its main ores are pyrolusite—a black, soft, granular oxide, and the rarer braunite—a manganese silicate. Rhodochrosite is a soft, pink manganese carbonate gem.

MERCURY, the only common metal that is normally liquid, is rare and constantly increasing in value. Mexico has soft, red cinnabar (mercury sulfide), a low-temperature mineral found in lavas.

ANTIMONY, a semimetal like arsenic, is used mainly as an alloy. Its only important ore is stibnite, a black compound of antimony and sulfur that forms long, needle-like crystals at low temperatures.

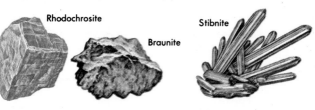

Rhodochrosite

Braunite

Stibnite

Mexican deposits of Iron

Mexican deposits of Mercury

MEXICAN GEMS are mainly of the quartz family—opal, amethyst, agate, jasper, some citrine, and rock crystal. Aquamarine and emerald are found, also garnet and gem topaz. Good jade is rare and not often offered for sale. Synthetic stones are common: alexandrite (green and red), ruby (red), sapphire (blue), and emerald (green) are sold, unmounted or in jewelry.

Opal in Matrix

cut opals

Amethyst crystal

cut amethyst

OPALS, a noncrystalline silica containing water, are perhaps the best of Mexico's gems. They range from common stones that reveal color only when wet to valuable fire opals. Most come from the state of Queretaro.

AMETHYST is a violet or purple crystalline quartz. Those of deep color are fine semiprecious stones. Pale or flawed stones are often mounted in silver. Found lining cavities in lava in the states of Queretaro and Guerrero.

TOPAZ is a fine Mexican gem, mostly yellowish or light brown, and nearly transparent. It is a complex fluosilicate of high-temperature veins. Brownish quartz is often sold as topaz. The two are difficult to tell apart.

JADE is a hard silicate mineral, green, gray, or bluish, often waxy, found as pebbles in stream beds. It was prized long before the Conquest. Ornaments 3,000 years old have been discovered. Beware of dyed onyx imitations.

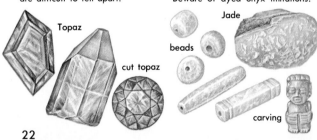

Topaz

cut topaz

Jade

beads

carving

PLANTS

For its size, Mexico offers an unusual variety of climates and an even greater range of landforms. The result is a bonanza of plants, ranging from stunted arctic species at the timberlines of high peaks to the giant trees of tropical rain forests. Over 10,000 species have been identified. Long before the Spanish came, Mexico had a prosperous agriculture. Indians gathered and cultivated plants for food, medicine, and other uses. Montezuma's gardens—reputedly a great collection of native plants—grew in what is now the Zocalo in Mexico City. Plants shown in this section were selected from Mexico's most important and conspicuous species.

MEXICAN PLANTS often have several local names in Spanish or in Indian languages. Sometimes the same name applies to different species. To avoid confusion, this book gives an acceptable English common name for each species, and a scientific name (pp. 155–156). This universally accepted Latin name is essential if you want more information about Mexican plants and animals.

FOR MORE ABOUT MEXICAN PLANTS, READ:

Barrett, Mary F., COMMON EXOTIC TREES OF S. FLORIDA. U. of Florida Press, Gainesville, Fla., 1956. Includes many introduced Mexican species.

Buggeman, L., TROPICAL PLANTS AND THEIR CULTIVATION. Crowell, N.Y., 1957. Fine color plates of native and introduced Mexican plants.

Clark, Phil, A GUIDE TO MEXICAN FLORA. Edit. Minutiae Mexicana, Mexico, D.F., 1964. A small, readable guide to common plants.

Martinez, Maximino, PLANTAS UTILES DE MEXICO (1936) and LAS PLANTAS MEDICINALES DE MEXICO (1944). Both published by the author, Mexico, D.F. Descriptions of plants and their uses. In Spanish.

Miranda, Faustino, LA VEGETACION DE CHIAPAS (2 vols.). Dept. Prensa y Turismo, Tuxtla, Mex., 1952. Authoritative survey of South Mexican plants. In Spanish.

O'Gorman, Helen, MEXICAN FLOWERING TREES AND PLANTS. Ammex. Assoc., Mexico, D.F., 1961. Large color plates of attractive species.

Pesman, M. Walter, MEET FLORA MEXICANA. Dale S. King, Globe, Ariz., 1962. A useful guide, arranged by plant zones.

Standley, Paul C., TREES AND SHRUBS OF MEXICO. Contr. U.S. Nat. Herb., G.P.O., Wash. D.C., 1920–26. Classic study in reprint.

MONTEZUMA BALDCYPRESS, or Ahuehuete, is Mexico's celebrated national tree. Under one, Cortes once wept in defeat. Grows 150 ft. high and (at Tule, near Oaxaca) 160 ft. around. Thin, drooping leaves fall in winter. Note round, brownish cones. Central and southern Mexico; widely planted, as in Chapultepec Park, Mexico City.

CONIFERS are typical of the limited, cold boreal zone and the much larger and more important pine-oak region. In addition to the species shown on these two pages, Douglas Fir (not a fir) occurs at high altitudes and several kinds of cypress grow in warmer areas. The still-abundant conifers are trees of major economic importance, furnishing timber, fuel, resins, and the tasty pine nuts.

JUNIPERS—several species, both shrubs and trees—grow in the north or in the mountains. Note Alligator Juniper's scaly leaves and angular twigs. Berry-like fruits are red or blue when ripe.

SACRED FIR is found mainly on high volcanic peaks. Slender, flat, blunt-tipped needles are 1 in. long. Cones upright; purple when ripe. A valuable timber tree with soft wood.

Alligator Juniper

Sacred Fir

PINES, most common Mexican conifers (39 species), are best identified by needles; usually in groups of three (yellow pines) 1 2 3 or five (white pines) 4 5 6 7 8.

MONTEZUMA PINE, the common pine of central and southern Mexico, has thin, drooping, 4–5-in. needles and 4–8-in. cones, also drooping. Trunk straight; dark, furrowed bark.

HARTWEG PINE, considered by some botanists to be a variety of the above, grows at higher altitudes (to timberline). Leaves and cones are relatively shorter. Cones drop when ripe.

MEXICAN WHITE PINE, found from Chihuahua south through Chiapas, has 4–8-in. needles that droop slightly. Cones, to 8 in. or more, are curved and have thick scales.

JALOCOTE PINE resembles Montezuma Pine but has 3 needles, over 6 in. long. Small dark cones persist on twigs. Central Mexico, and widely planted.

LUMHOLTZ PINE (*Piño Triste*), from Chihuahua to Tepic, has needles 8–12 in. long; drooping branches. Cones dull brown, 2–3 in. long. Thick, scaly bark darkens with age.

CHIHUAHUA PINE, dominant pine of Chihuahua Mts., has short, stiff, slender needles, 3–4 to a bundle; 2–3-in. cones ripen in 3 years. Trees 30–50 ft. high; bark ridged.

AZTEC PINE, 60–90 ft., has long, stiff needles and clusters of small brown cones. Yields turpentine and pitch. Aztec priests burned the resin as incense.

MEXICAN PINYON PINES (6 species) have short needles in clusters of 2 and 3. Heavy flat cones yield pine or pinyon nuts—tasty and often available in markets.

25

TEMPERATE ZONE TREES and shrubs in Mexico are a varied lot because the temperate climates are equally varied. Cooler temperate regions include the pine-oak forests, the high boreal forests (mainly conifers), and the upper parts of tropical cloud forests. The warmer temperate areas are mainly chaparral and mesquite scrublands in addition to much of what we call "desert." The cooler temperate areas include many trees and shrubs that are commonly seen north of the border in southern and western U.S. In addition to the three species below, temperate plants include the pines (p. 24) and oaks (p. 27) and species of ash, sycamore, box elder, sweet and sour gums, hornbeam, beech, basswood, dogwood, hawthorn, elderberry, and many others.

HANDFLOWER TREE, once prized by the Aztecs and long considered rare, is widely known and planted for its unusual flowers, which resemble a red hand. Note the long-stemmed, large, hairy, sycamore-shaped leaves. Grows 30–50 ft. high, from Oaxaca into southern Mexico.

RAMROD TREE, a relative of the elms, may rise nearly 300 ft., with upturned branches; its straight trunk is covered with scaly bark. Recognized by its sharp, uneven, toothed, alternate leaves. Fruits are small, flattened, and hairy. Common in cool mountain forests.

TREE FERNS are true ferns, 15–30 ft. tall, locally common in cloud forests. Fronds, 6–8 ft. long, begin as "fiddleheads" and slowly unfold. These, and a thin, dark trunk, marked by leaf scars, make identification simple. About 6 species from Veracruz south.

MEXICAN OAKS (over 100 species) are important trees over much of Mexico, at elevations above 5,000 feet. Most species fit into two rough categories—the *encino* or live (evergreen) oaks, with small leathery leaves that fall gradually so the tree is never bare; and the *roble* (deciduous) oaks, trees with larger leaves.

ENCINO OAKS

EMORY OAK, widespread, medium-sized, and abundant tree of northern Mexico, has thick, short-stemmed, leathery leaves 1–2 in. long, with spiny teeth. Acorns mature in 2 years.

MEXICAN OAK is found farther south in central Mexico. Leaves are small, thick, hairy below, wrinkled, with a slightly rolled edge. Acorns, small and bitter, are half covered in a rounded cup.

NET-LEAF OAK has heavy twigs and short-stemmed, wide, thick, spiny leaves; blue-gray above, hairy-brown below. Veins are heavy, raised. Small, pointed acorns in a deep rounded cup.

WRINKLE-LEAF OAK has stout twigs, small buds, and large, heavy, wrinkled leaves with shallow lobes. Lack spiny points, hairy below. Acorns small, in a shallow cup.

ROBLE OAKS

27

ARID-LAND TREES and shrubs have spread into areas that are variously called chaparral, mesquite, and desert. Rainfall in all is low and poorly distributed, but many plants in addition to the cacti (pp. 30–31) thrive in these dry areas. Most of the trees and shrubs have small leaves, which may be shed during drought. The desert of Baja California is most striking; its unusual species include the nearly conical, almost inconceivable Boojum Tree. Some typical desert trees and shrubs follow.

CREOSOTE BUSH spots the dry lands of central and northern Mexico, often as the dominant plant. Grows 4–6 ft. high with paired dull leaves and (after rains) masses of yellow flowers that mature into white, hairy fruits. Tarbush, a smaller, rounded, and even more common shrub, is almost a solid mass of yellow flower heads when it blooms in summer.

OCOTILLO rises as clumps of green, thorny wands, 6–15 ft. high, in the northern deserts. Small oval leaves unfold after rains but soon wither. Spring flowers form a tapering red cluster, conspicuous at a distance. Sometimes planted as a hedge.

ACACIAS, native and widespread (some 60 species in Mexico), form a self-contained group within the pea family. Two species are illustrated here. Sweet Acacia (1), seen almost everywhere, has fragrant flowers and fine thorns. Catclaw Acacia (2), of desert washes in the north, has large hooked thorns and catkins of pale-yellow flowers. Most acacias have twice-compounded leaves. Fruits are beanlike. Many yield gums that have local or commercial value.

MESQUITE is a shrub or small tree, widespread on arid lands. The greenish twigs, with pairs of short, straight spines, bear bicompound leaves of many small leaflets. Greenish-yellow catkins develop into knobby, brown, edible beans, about 6 in. long. Screwbean Mesquite, a very similar species, has tightly twisted beans.

PALO VERDE, also in the pea family, is a spiny, 25-ft. tree of drier places. Its green stems bear the small, bicompound leaves for only a short period of the year. The attractive 5-petaled flowers are yellow and fragrant, appearing suddenly and in great profusion. Fruits are beanlike, 2–4 in. long.

DESERT WILLOW, with showy, tubular, lilac-and-white flowers, is not a willow but a shrub, related to catalpas. Leaves are narrow, like willow. Common in washes or in sandy areas of northern Mexico, south to Durango. Occasionally planted as an ornamental. The fruits are long, slender pods containing many small, winged seeds.

LIGNUMVITAE is a widespread native tree of semiarid areas; small (15–20 ft.) with gray bark and small compound leaves. It may be unnoticed until, in early spring, it bursts into bloom with bright-blue, 5-petaled flowers that cover the entire tree. Its very hard, heavy wood is still prized for its color and texture.

MORNING GLORY TREES (some 30 species) occur in central and northern Mexico as small trees or shrubs with thick, gray, hairy twigs, long leaves, and gray bark. In winter, after the leaves are shed, large white, tubular flowers appear at the ends of stout twigs. All parts of the plant are poisonous when eaten.

29

CACTI are a family of plants well adapted to desert life. Lack of leaves, extensive roots, a waxy epidermis, water-storing stems, shaped with a minimum of surface, and plenty of spines make them successful. Many have large, showy flowers. The fruits of larger cacti and the young "pads" of prickly pear (*Opuntia*) species are edible and nutritious. Mexico is a paradise of cacti. Species number in the hundreds. On these pages are some of the more common and spectacular kinds. See also the agaves, p. 32, and yuccas, p. 34.

1. **NOPAL** is a common flat-stemmed prickly pear (*Opuntia*) of hillsides and yards. The fruit and young pads are eaten. This is the cactus on the Mexican flag.

2. **BARREL CACTI** of northern Mexico are water-storing species 3–5 ft. high, studded with curved spines. Yellow or reddish flowers circle the crown. Fruit yellow.

3. **PIPESTEM CACTUS,** also an *Opuntia*, has slender fleshy stems at right angles to the branches; long, straight thorns, small yellow flowers, and bright-red fruits.

4. **CHOLLA,** another *Opuntia*, may grow 10 ft. tall. Its woody network trunk and joints are covered with fleshy tubercules. Flowers purple; fruit yellow.

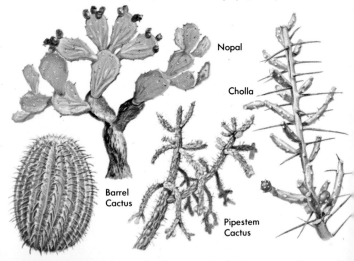

Nopal

Cholla

Barrel Cactus

Pipestem Cactus

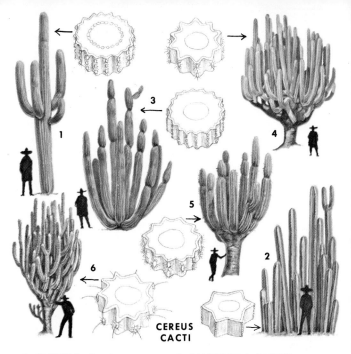

CEREUS CACTI

1. SAGUARO of northern Mexico has a single 30–40-ft. trunk with upright branches, each with 12–24 ribs. Flowers white, tubular; fruit egg-shaped, bright red.

2. ORGANPIPE is a common cactus 10–20 ft. high, branching upright at ground level. Planted as single uprights for fences. Stems with 5–7 vertical ribs.

3. TETETZO grows 35–55 ft. tall with a few small branches high above the ground. Low and rounded ribs, 13–15, around the stem. Central Mexico.

4. CANDELABRA CACTUS similar to Organpipe but taller (to 30 ft.) has erect branches. Stems with about 10 sharp ridges. Flowers white. Central Mexico.

5. GIANT CACTUS, to 35 ft., is common in northwestern Mexico. Trunk splits into branches, with 11–15 ribs and large spines. Brown hairs around flowers.

6. HAIRBRUSH CACTUS, named for its spiny fruits, branches 5–6 ft. from the ground. Branches very spiny, with 10–11 ribs; flowers purple and white.

31

AGAVES, (amaryllis family) are Mexico's most typical plants. Of some 400 species, about 185 grow here, preferring the drier regions. Agaves are also called mogueys or century plants, though their life span (they die after blooming) is rarely more than 10 years. Agaves bear tubular flowers on a tall stalk when the plant matures. Most flower stalks are branched. In others, the flowers (usually in pairs) form a tight spike. Agaves provide food, drink (fermented), and three kinds of tough fibers.

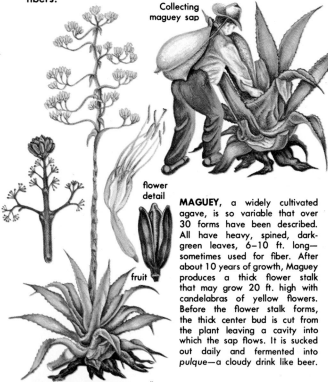

Collecting maguey sap

flower detail

fruit

MAGUEY, a widely cultivated agave, is so variable that over 30 forms have been described. All have heavy, spined, dark-green leaves, 6–10 ft. long—sometimes used for fiber. After about 10 years of growth, Maguey produces a thick flower stalk that may grow 20 ft. high with candelabras of yellow flowers. Before the flower stalk forms, the thick center bud is cut from the plant leaving a cavity into which the sap flows. It is sucked out daily and fermented into *pulque*—a cloudy drink like beer.

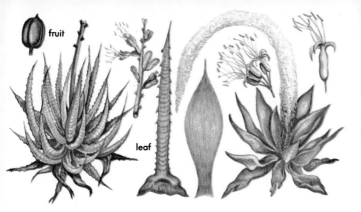

LECHEGUILLA, a common agave of the northern deserts, is one of about 50 species with flowers in a spike. Flower stalk 8–20 ft. high. Leaves thin, blue-green, with pungent spines. A source of istle fiber.

HENEQUEN, planted mile after mile in the dry tropics, is the agave that produces the once-important sisal fiber. The blue-gray leaves, with conical spines, are cut from the bottom.

DROOPING AGAVE, better described by its Spanish name, *Cola de Leon* (Lion's Tail), is a less common agave of the Chihuahua Desert. Blooms form a drooping spike. Leaves thin, smooth, and spineless. Short trunk.

MESCAL, or Cabbage Agave, is easily recognized by its rounded, compact form and thick, wide, spiny leaves. The flower stalk rises 10–12 ft. high, with yellowish, red-tipped flowers.

YUCCAS, typical plants of semiarid lands and deserts, should not be confused with agaves (pp. 32–33), cacti (pp. 30–31), or other similar plants of the lily family (p. 35). Some 40 species of yuccas grow in Mexico. Nearly half are treelike. The rest grow on the ground as rosettes of spiked leaves with a tall central flower stalk. Yuccas are lilies with stiff, narrow leaves ending in daggers. The edges are smooth but fibrous. Large spikes of white flowers grow on upright stalks. Unlike the agaves, yuccas do not die after flowering.

IZOTE, with a 10–12-ft. trunk, is a common tree yucca of dry central and northern Mexico. Leaves narrow, 3 ft. long. Flowers, cream or white.

AMOLE YUCCA, of arid northern Mexico, grows to 20 ft. tall, with a large root that may be used as soap. Flowers and fruit are edible. Stalk and flower cluster upright.

OTHER YUCCAS are similar to the two illustrated below, except for about 20 smaller, trunkless species. Identification is difficult. Check details of fruits and flowers, plant form and size.

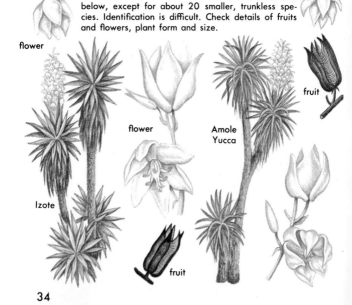

flower

Izote

flower

Amole Yucca

fruit

fruit

YUCCA-LIKE PLANTS

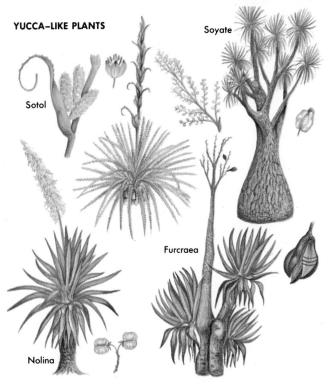

Soyate

Sotol

Furcraea

Nolina

SOTOL has narrow, spiny leaves with a broad, spoonlike base. Flower stalk (6–12 ft.) bears small creamy flowers. The short trunk is roasted; leaf bases eaten or fermented into a strong drink.

NOLINA (12 species), with a short unbranched trunk, grows from Sonora to Baja California. Leaves, long and coarse. Flowers small, white, or greenish. Papery seed cases; three winged seeds.

SOYATE is an open-branched tree (to 30 ft.) with a dark, scaly trunk and spongy wood. Leaves smooth, slender, drooping. Small creamy flowers in short spikes. Central and southern Mexico.

FURCRAEA is related to the agaves. Nine Mexican species are usually treelike, often unbranched, with a large flowering stalk 10–12 ft. tall. Long leaves yield *pita*—a fiber very much like sisal.

PALMS can be seen in most parts of tropical and warm temperate Mexico. About 60 species are native, and a number of exotic palms are cultivated. Palms are found in the river bottoms of the northern deserts, but they are more abundant in the dry forests along the Pacific coast and in the savannas and rain forests of the tropical lowlands. Most palms are treelike, with large palmate (hand-shaped) or pinnate (feather-shaped) leaves that, in some, may be 20 ft. long. The "woody" trunks are tough and fibrous. Small, inconspicuous flowers appear in long, stalked clusters. Fruits, often berry-like, are eaten by man and by wildlife. Palm leaves are used for thatching, making hats and mats; trunks are used in building; flower buds and fruits are eaten.

COCONUTS are so widely distributed in the tropics their origin is uncertain. Nuts, carried by ocean currents, started Mexican coconut palms long before Europeans arrived. Now coconuts grow commonly along low shores, where average temperatures are in the 60's or higher. Coconut plantations—a small, local industry—are found in the Isthmus and along the warm coasts. Coconuts grow 20–30 ft. tall, and take about 7 years to mature and bear fruit. Nuts are cut green for "milk" or cut when ripe for their meat.

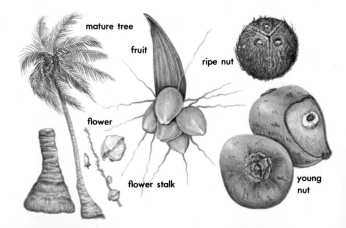

mature tree

fruit

ripe nut

flower

flower stalk

young nut

SABAL *(Palma reál)* grows 30–50 ft. high and forms sparse groves in savannas and coastal plains. Trunks of young trees are covered with bases of leaves. Leaves used for thatching; small black fruits are eaten by birds and small mammals. Flowers, in thin clusters, are small and green. Several species of Sabal grow in Mexico.

COHUNE PALM is a tall and handsome tree of the tropical lowlands. It is usually left to grow when patches are cleared for farming. Needs good soil and adequate water. Fruits and seeds are eaten. Leaves, which lack spines, are used in weaving and in making hats. Large, spreading leaves and a short trunk are characteristic.

WASHINGTON PALM is a large species growing to 70 ft. high, with a stout trunk and a terminal cluster of spiny, fan-shaped leaves. Grows mainly in Sonora and Baja California, but is cultivated widely. Hanging clusters of tiny flowers mature into small dark fruits. Smooth trunk is usually covered by layers of dead leaves.

CHAMAEDOREA, a group of small, delicate palms, includes about 25 species—nearly half of all Mexican palms. Most are slender trees of southern Mexico's rain forests. These palms lack spines; trunks are slender; leaves feathery. Flowers and small fruits, in clusters. This group has not been studied sufficiently.

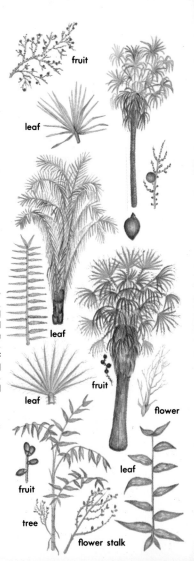

fruit

leaf

leaf

leaf

fruit

flower

leaf

fruit

tree

flower stalk

TROPICAL TREES are found in only about a quarter of Mexico. At high altitudes in the tropics, some of the trees are temperate species (p. 26). In the tropics are the largest, most spectacular, and most important Mexican trees. Some form the rain forests, which are perpetually green. Some are typical of the drier areas, where winter drought causes the trees to shed. Some (especially palms, pp. 36–37) grow in the open tropical savannas. On these pages (38–40) are samples of native tropical trees.

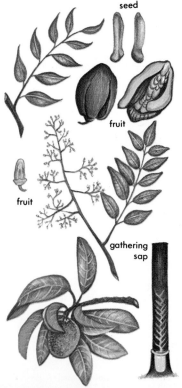

seed

fruit

fruit

gathering sap

MAHOGANY wood is prized for furniture and finishing. The rough, gray-barked tree that produces it grows well over 100 ft. tall in the rain forests. The leaves are compound, with 3–5 stalked, oval, and opposite leaflets. The small flowers grow in loose clusters and form unusual pods that open to drop the broad-winged seeds.

CEDRO, or Cigarbox Tree, is a close relative of Mahogany and has similar leaves and flowers. The leaflets, however, are long and narrow, and the fruits are much smaller. Grows over 100 ft. tall with smooth gray bark. Most large trees are gone—cut for their fine-grained, reddish wood—once universally used for cigar boxes.

CHICLE, or Sapodilla, grows 60 ft. tall. Known also as the "chewing gum" tree. The latex sap is gathered and boiled before shipping. Indians chewed the gum and ate the oval, brown fruit, with a pear-like flavor. Leaves are simple, long, and shiny; flowers, small and brown. The hard, brown wood was used in Mayan temples.

Strangler Fig

fruit

flower

Gourd Tree

seed pod

Ceiba

Lipstick Tree

fruits

FIGS (about 25 species) have simple, leathery leaves and milky sap. Flowers small; fruits edible. Birds drop seeds of strangler figs into rough bark or palm thatch. The aerial roots of the seedling wrap around host tree, and work down to the ground.

CEIBA, or Kapok Tree, is another giant, growing over 100 ft. tall, with a buttressed trunk, smooth gray bark, and stout, spiny twigs. Leaves, palmately compound, drop in winter. Greenish-red flowers develop into large seed pods, full of white fibers (kapok).

GOURD (CALABASH) TREE is a low, spreading tree of the tropical savannas. One kind has simple leaves; the other has 3 leaflets, forming a cross. The large yellow flowers produce gourds, up to a foot in diameter, that are used as containers.

LIPSTICK TREE is a shrub or small tree that yields a strong, orange-red dye, now used to give butter and cheese that "rich" look. Leaves alternate, coarse, heart-shaped. The large, pinkish, 5-petaled flowers give rise to burlike fruits with pigmented pulp.

39

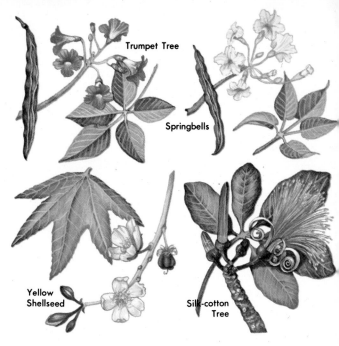

Trumpet Tree

Springbells

Yellow Shellseed

Silk-cotton Tree

TRUMPET TREE, a small member of the catalpa family, is covered in spring with clusters of pale violet-pink flowers that mature into long pods. Leaves, palmately compound, grow opposite, after the flowers fall. Common in southern Mexico.

YELLOW SHELLSEED, a small tree found from Sonora south, has a dozen Mexican names, all referring to the large, golden-yellow flowers set off by brown sepals. Fruit is large and round; brown when mature. Leaves, palmately compound, appear after flowers.

SPRINGBELLS, closely related to the Trumpet Tree, has flowers in rich-yellow clusters. The palmate leaves (5–7 leaflets) and the pods are also similar. This large tree is often planted for its delightful flowers. It is also planted as a timber tree.

SILK-COTTON TREE bears large, pink or white flowers with numerous stamens and stout, recurved petals. Leaves, palmately compound with broad leaflets, do not unfold till after tree has flowered. The fruit has small seeds with heavy fiber, like Ceiba's (p. 39).

INTRODUCED PLANTS flourish in Mexico's mild yet varied climate, which provides many habitats where exotic species grow well. Tropical and subtropical lands all over the world have contributed to the Mexican flora, and plants from Mexico are grown worldwide where soil and climate permit. Introduced plants yield timber and much of Mexico's food; they also help to control erosion. Some are beautiful ornamentals. See pp. 44–45 for herbaceous plants and pp. 50–51 for fruits. Many native plants have been improved horticulturally and are widely cultivated for food, for medicine, and for decorative uses.

woody fruit

fruit

EUCALYPTUS trees from Australia have been too widely planted, as the trees have limited value. One common kind provides roadside shade and makes a good windbreak. Note the narrow, aromatic leaves; squared, woody fruits; light peeling bark.

PERUVIAN PEPPERTREE is another widespread tree of limited value except for shade. The drooping twigs bear long compound leaves with alternating leaflets. Open clusters of yellowish flowers become red, dry berries. All parts are strongly aromatic.

41

seed pod

OLEANDER, a widely planted Mediterranean shrub, grows rapidly. It has simple, heavy, pointed leaves in clusters of three. The white or pink flowers are in terminal clusters. Fruits are long, narrow pods. All parts are poisonous if eaten.

BOUGAINVILLEA is a vine from Brazil that may be trimmed as a shrub. Its small creamy flowers are surrounded by showy, orange-red to purple bracts. Leaves are simple, alternate; twigs bear sharp spines. Its rapid growth makes it a common ornamental.

AUSTRALIAN PINE, or Beefwood, is a large, odd tree from Australia. Not a pine, but related to hickories, it has small, scaly leaves on thin, drooping twigs that give it a piney look. Wood is hard and tough. These fast-growing trees are used for shade.

TROPICAL ALMOND is not the true almond, though its nuts are edible. This attractive East Indian tree with angular, spreading branches is widely planted. Note the broad-tipped, alternate leaves, with wavy edges. Flowers, small and white, in open clusters.

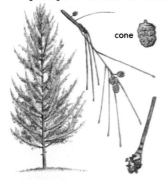

cone

nut

FRANGIPANI, or Plumeria (5 species), is commonly planted. The large 5-petaled, very fragrant, cream or pink flowers open in spring, often before leaves appear. Leaves are oval and thick, with distinctive veins and a milky sap.

ORCHID TREE (at least 20 species from India and the East Indies) is a member of the pea family. It has large white, pink, or violet flowers that vaguely resemble orchids. The small trees have a light bark and simple, round, alternate, cleft leaves.

JACARANDA, from Brazil, has loose clusters of tubular, sky-blue flowers that appear mainly in spring as the bicompound leaves are unfolding. Fruits are brown, oval wafers. Some may hang on the twigs until next year's flowers appear.

ROYAL POINCIANA, from Madagascar, has become a symbol of the Caribbean and is planted in the warmer parts of Mexico. It grows low with a flat, spreading crown, large bicompound leaves, and clusters of orange-red, open flowers. Fruits are heavy pods.

fruit

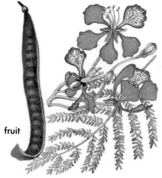

fruit

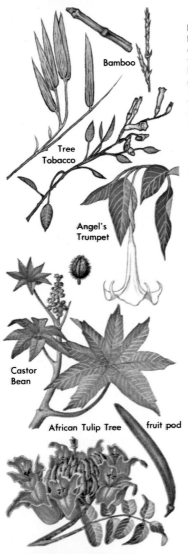

BAMBOOS are fast-growing members of the grass family. The species range in height from a few feet to over 100. Widely planted, bamboos grow from an underground rootstock. Those of the tropics form dense clumps. Note the tall, smooth stems with thin, grasslike leaves growing from swollen nodes.

Scores of species, native and introduced, are used for house construction, fences, furniture, baskets, rafts and boats, fishing rods, and as ornamentals.

TREE TOBACCO, a close relative of the tobacco plant, is a 20-ft. tree from Argentina, now naturalized and abundant in warm parts of Mexico. Leaves simple and alternate; flowers tubular, greenish or pale yellow.

ANGEL'S TRUMPET (Peruvian) refers not only to the shape of the large white flowers but also to the fact that eating the plant may produce the angel's call. Related to Jimson Weed, this attractive, poisonous tree is widely planted.

CASTOR BEAN is shrubby, 10–15 ft. tall, with stout branches. Leaves are large, palmate, often bronze. Fruits are clusters of small burs, each containing 3 mottled seeds from which castor oil is made. Poisonous.

AFRICAN TULIP TREE has clusters of large, orange-red flowers that emerge from a flat spiral of hairy buds. Fruits are heavy pods. This rapidly growing tree of medium and low areas has hairy, compound leaves with 9–13 leaflets.

FLOWERS, both annuals and perennials as well as flowering trees and shrubs, abound in Mexico. The Aztecs had a God of Flowers (Xochipilli), and flowers were cultivated long before the Spaniards came. Today every town market still has them, cut or potted. Many flowers grown in Mexico, such as calla lilies, hibiscus, and fuchsias, come from other warm areas. Many Mexican and Central American species have been developed under cultivation. Dahlias, cosmos, verbenas, zinnias, petunias, ageratum, marigolds, lantana, and poinsettias are just a few of the well-known Mexican plants.

fruit

YELLOW PRICKLY-POPPY, common in all drier parts of Mexico, is an attractive but annoying weed. The dissected leaves are needle-tipped, as are the stems. Flowers are usually yellow, but some are white.

HUMMINGBIRD BUSH is easily spotted with its red, tubular, double-lipped flowers that form a loose, erect spike. The bush, 3 or 4 ft. tall, has small, hairy, opposite leaves. Several species grow along dry roadsides.

CASSIAS, a large group of shrubby and herbaceous plants of the pea family, include some 50 Mexican species. All have yellow flowers and compound leaves. Common in warm, dry areas, where they often form thickets.

BRITTLEBUSH is a shrubby composite with yellow flower heads and small, hairy, alternate leaves. Grows on dry hillsides. Stems produce a clear resin. A score or more of similar composite shrubs are found in Mexico.

SHELLFLOWER, or Tigridia, is a handsome iris with petals and three sepals that range from white to yellow, pink, and orange with dark spots at the center. Common through central Mexico in fields and open woods. The Aztecs cooked and ate the bulbs.

TUBEROSE, native to southern Mexico, is now widely cultivated for the delicate colors (white to pink) of the waxen flowers, but more for its rich, penetrating perfume. Flowers are both single and double. Often sold in markets.

ZEPHYR LILIES, a group of native bulbous flowers of drier areas, bloom after the summer rains; hence their other name: rain lilies. They have creamy-white to pink flowers that darken with age, and long slender leaves.

JACOBEAN LILY is native to central Mexico and is widely cultivated for its large, bright-red flowers, over 6 in. in diameter. Blooms in summer. Shiny, dark-green leaves are long and narrow.

SPIDER LILIES are another widespread group, common in moist areas and also cultivated. A number of species all have white flowers with very narrow petals and sepals. Light-green leaves are long and thick.

DAHLIA is the national flower of Mexico, where it has been developed from a simple wild plant of the highlands into thousands of cultivated forms. Tree dahlias of southern Mexico grow 12 ft. tall. The wild dahlia has pink petals and a yellow center.

ZINNIAS form another native Mexican group, common in fields and open places at middle altitudes. The flowers range from white through yellow, orange, red, and purple—all with yellow centers. Leaves opposite. Five species are large and shrubby.

MARIGOLDS and calendulas, both native, were known to the Indians as flowers of the dead. Even today do not take them as house gifts. Both are now cultivated in many horticultural forms. Though Mexican in origin, marigolds are classified as French or African.

COSMOS are a group of native herbs and semiwoody (2–5 ft.) plants, with opposite, deeply cut leaves and with flower heads that range from white to yellow, pink, and purple. Found at middle altitudes. Often seen in cultivation.

POINSETTIA is widely used for Christmas decoration in Mexico, but here it is also a wild native shrub, 5–20 ft. tall. Flowers are small and yellow, set amid scarlet bracts. Named after the U.S. ambassador who popularized the plant in the 1820's.

AIR PLANTS (epiphytes) grow on trees, rocks, poles, and rooftops in central and southern Mexico. Some kinds live on evergreens in the cool, moist alpine forests; others thrive in the humid lowlands. In spite of this manner of growth, none of these plants is a parasite. All manufacture their own food. Their elevated position may give epiphytes better access to light and moisture and free them from the intense competition at ground level. Some species catch rain in their leaves. All absorb moisture from fog and mist. They sometimes cover branches so densely that the added weight causes limbs to break in a windstorm. Epiphytes include species of mosses, lichens, ferns, and a multitude of flowering plants. The best-known epiphytes are members of the orchid and pineapple families (p. 49).

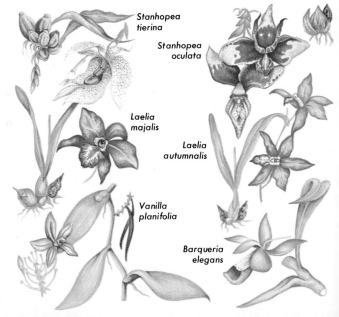

Stanhopea
tierina

Stanhopea
oculata

Laelia
majalis

Laelia
autumnalis

Vanilla
planifolia

Barqueria
elegans

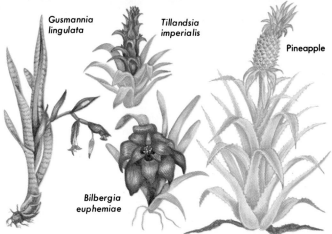

Gusmannia lingulata

Tillandsia imperialis

Pineapple

Bilbergia euphemiae

ORCHIDS (left) form the largest, best-known, and most attractive family of plants. Over 600 species are native to Mexico. Most are epiphytes, growing from San Luis Potosi south through Chiapas. Many orchid species thrive in the highlands, where they are more abundant than in the tropical rain forests. Most, but not all, have large colorful flowers, as in Mexican species of *Laelia, Cattleya, Stanhopea,* and *Oncidium.* Gardens often include orchids.

Some Mexican species have been used to develop even more attractive hybrids. Many epiphytic orchids have a thickened stem (pseudo-bulb) that stores food. The Vanilla Orchid, a vinelike species, is grown commercially in the tropical lowlands. For more details on Mexican orchids, read Norman P. Wright's *Orquídes de Mexico,* Editorial Fournier, Mexico, D.F., 1958. It is in Spanish and English.

THE PINEAPPLE FAMILY (above) includes hundreds of species besides the common cultivated kind that produces such excellent fruit in the southern lowlands. Included are many epiphytes that pass under the label of bromeliad, the name for the entire family.

Travelers usually see more bromeliads than orchids. They line branches and make conspicuous clumps. Many have rosettes of long, thick, narrow, pointed leaves, sometimes tipped with red. From this clump grows the long flower stalk, some with red and purple bracts. The most attractive Mexican bromeliad is Guacamaya *(Tillandsia imperialis),* often used as a Christmas decoration. Other species of *Tillandsia* are common, including the misnamed Spanish Moss. Bromeliad epiphytes also include species of *Billbergia, Aechmea,* and *Guzmannia.* Many are difficult to identify and lack common names.

49

FOOD AND CROP PLANTS outrank all others in importance. Their prodigious products overflow the markets. Besides such well-known fruits as apples, pears, peaches, grapes, melons, and oranges, you will see many less familiar tropical kinds. You will want to identify these and the equally interesting vegetables, and with reasonable concern (p. 5), you can safely try them.

AVOCADO, a native of tropical Mexico, appears in varied forms—some with rough skins, some with smooth. Local avocados (several varieties) are usually small, but newer hybrids may weigh a pound or more. Eaten in salads and in *guacamolé*.

MANGO, from India, reached Mexico in the 1700's and was soon common in warmer areas. The old-type fruits, small and with a turpentine flavor, are being replaced by newer, large varieties that are praised as one of the tastiest fruits.

LIMON, the small, greenish citrus fruit used in many drinks and dishes, is not a lemon but a lime with a welcome tart flavor. Widely grown, it is tolerant of poor soils. Oranges, tangerines, and other citrus fruits are sold in the markets.

MAMEY is a Caribbean tree planted in warm, moist southern Mexico. The fruit is shaped like a peach and 4 to 7 in. in diameter. Skin is rough, reddish brown; flesh, yellow and juicy. Used in preserves or sweets.

ZAPOTE is an Aztec word for soft, sweet fruits. With sundry adjectives, the name is applied to a score of unrelated plants. The more common and conspicuous zapote fruits are shown below. Among the others is Mamey (p. 50), often called *Zapote de Santo Domingo*.

YELLOW ZAPOTE, usually green in the market, is roughly peach-shaped, 3–4 in., with a hooked tip. Soft when ripe, the creamy flesh has a pleasant flavor. Seeds, 3–4, are large and dark. Fruit allegedly makes one sleepy or drunk.

BLACK ZAPOTE is a persimmon and, like the native U.S. species, is about 2 in. in diameter—much smaller than the cultivated Japanese persimmons. The skin is dark green. Flesh, soft and black, is eaten fresh or is made into preserves or a tasty liquor.

WHITE ZAPOTE belongs in the same family as oranges and is about the same size and shape, but with a thin greenish skin and a tart creamy pulp. Seeds, 3–5, dark brown. The fruit has the same reputation as Yellow Zapote.

CHICLE ZAPOTE, or Sapodilla, the fruit of the Chicle Tree (p. 38), may be round or oval (2–4 in. diameter). Skin is rough, reddish brown; flesh brownish, with the texture of a ripe Seckel Pear. Eaten fresh, excellent flavor. Seeds are shiny black.

MARMALADE FRUIT will also be called Mamey in the market, causing confusion (p. 50). This oval fruit (eaten fresh) is more commonly seen, since it ships well. Skin a rich red-brown; flesh paler, soft and sweet. Seed, large and dark.

PAPAYA is the fruit of a treelike plant that bears for 2 or 3 years. Female "trees" have fruit in all stages of development along the upper trunk. Melon-sized fruits are eaten fresh (with *limon*). The dried milky sap is used as a meat tenderizer.

SOURSOP belongs to a group that provides half a dozen tasty fruits in and near the tropics. Oval fruit, up to 5 pounds, is green, with fleshy spines. The white juicy pulp is eaten fresh or is used in jellies, ice cream, and drinks.

CUSTARD APPLE, or Chirimoya, has light-greenish, warty fruits, 3–4-in. diameter. Very soft when ripe, with a tasty creamy pulp and a good many black seeds. Fruit is good fresh and is also used in local ice cream.

GUAVAS bear round, yellow fruits the size of large plums, with yellow or pink flesh and numerous hard white seeds. Used mainly as preserves and in guava pastes. Other kinds have smaller, red fruits, all with a sweet-sour flavor.

BREADFRUIT, the famous tree of the South Pacific, has been introduced into Mexico. Fruits are seen mainly in smaller markets in the south. The large, round, warty fruits (8–10-in. diameter) have a yellowish flesh—and not much flavor.

TUNAS, or Cactus Apples, are the fruits of several species of prickly pear (Nopal, p. 30). Spines are rubbed off, and the oval yellow, red, or purple fruits, 2–4 in. long, are peeled and eaten fresh. The sweet, juicy pulp contains many small seeds.

TAMARIND is a large tree from India. Its beanlike fruits, with a hard brown skin, are rich in acids and sugar, giving them a sweet-sour flavor. The dark pulp is eaten fresh and is also used in making drinks and preserves.

PINE NUTS are the seeds of several pinyon pines (p. 25) found mainly in northern Mexico. The small, hard-shelled seeds are marketed intact or shelled. The soft, sweet, pinkish kernels have a delicate flavor that is unique.

COCONUTS are abundant in southern Mexico and in the coastal belts (p. 36). The large, green or brown nuts are offered in markets and at roadside stands—the green nuts as coco de agua for drinking; the brown mature fruits for milk and for the tasty meat.

COCOA BEANS come from the oval (10–12 in.) fruits of the Cacao Tree. The brownish beans are taken from the pulp and dried in the sun. Aztecs used the beans for money. Now they go to make cocoa for drinks, and chocolate for candies and ice cream.

COFFEE is an important crop of the southern and central highlands. Each red fruit contains a pair of beans. These are processed, sacked, and shipped to market. Strongly flavored Mexican blends are available and are worth trying.

JAMAICA (Roselle) is a hibiscus, grown for its reddish seed cases that are boiled to make a tasty, acid drink. Jamaica is also used in jams and jellies and was once used to color and flavor rum. Plant grows 5–7 ft. high, with yellow flowers.

Ejotes

Frijol

Chiles

Flor de Calabaza

Chicharo

Tomates

Rabano

Papalosi

Nopal

Quelites

Chayotes

Huitlacoche

VEGETABLES abound in Mexican markets. They come in daily by truck or burro and surpass, in variety, those seen in the U.S.

Many are familiar: potatoes (several small kinds), tomatoes (many kinds and shapes, including green husk tomatoes), carrots, cucumbers, onions, cabbage, peas, radishes (several kinds), lettuce, watercress, chili peppers (all sizes, shapes, colors, and potencies), peanuts, greens, beans (fresh and dried), wild mushrooms (in season), and all sorts of herbs.

Most of the less familiar market vegetables have been used in Mexico since pre-Hispanic times. Some shown above are *nopal,* tender cactus pods—boiled or fried; *chayote,* a small climbing squash; *papalosi,* a form of cress used in salads; *quelites,* a small-leaved vegetable, prepared like spinach, and *huitlacoche,* corn ears covered with fungus (corn smut), a delicacy cooked with peppers, onions, and tomatoes. At least a dozen other minor vegetables appear in markets.

ANIMALS

Species for species, Mexico surpasses the rest of North America in most classes of vertebrates. Northern Mexico is home to many groups, which also occur in southwestern U.S. To the south, tropical species fill a number of ecological niches. Invertebrates are omitted, except the few below. See other Golden Guides for marine invertebrates, fishes, reptiles, birds, and mammals that range south into Mexico. Most species illustrated here are not found north of the Rio Grande.

LAND INVERTEBRATES in Mexico (mainly insects) run into many thousands of species. Most of them ignore man. Those that are bothersome are well known: bees, wasps, ants, conenose bugs, lice, chiggers and ticks, and a few spiders. In the northern desert, watch for centipedes and scorpions. Centipedes can give a painful, slow-healing bite. Scorpions sting painfully with their tail. The sting of a small yellow species (illustrated) has been fatal to small children. Large spiders, including tarantulas, are not dangerous. The Black Widow, a smaller spider, is venomous.

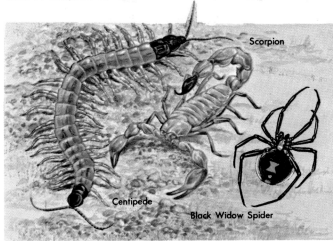

Scorpion

Centipede

Black Widow Spider

FISHES abound along Mexico's 6,300 miles of shoreline, and in lakes and rivers. Commercial fishing (p. 154) is for tuna, shrimp, snapper, and some smaller species. Mexico's game fish bring sportfishermen to Gulf and Pacific ports. Here is a sample of Mexican fishes from about 50 marine species sought by sportsmen. See also the Golden Guides FISHES and FISHING.

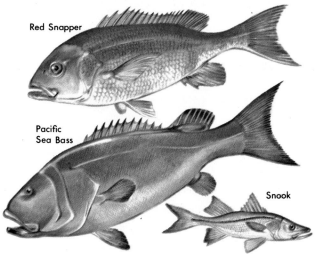

Red Snapper

Pacific Sea Bass

Snook

RED SNAPPER is common in the Gulf of Mexico. Larger fish, up to 3 ft., are caught in deep water. Smaller ones and several other species of snappers are found along shore, where they are caught with live baits. Snappers feed on small fish, crabs, and shrimp. Red Snapper (*huachinango*) is prized as a food fish of fine flavor and is served in most restaurants with local sauces.

PACIFIC SEA BASSES include several species: one, the Giant Sea Bass, may reach 600 lbs. Several smaller species are caught off rocky shores. All are game fish and are good eating.

SNOOK, found along both Mexican coasts, are caught in bays and inlets, sometimes in fresh water. Note the protruding lower jaw, the dark lateral line. Average 5 lbs., and up to 50 lbs.

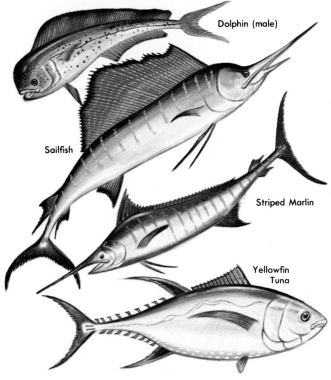

Dolphin (male)

Sailfish

Striped Marlin

Yellowfin Tuna

DOLPHINS are fast fish of the open seas, often seen chasing smaller fish at the surface. Colors are iridescent. Note long dorsal fins, and the high forehead of the male. Length to 6 ft.

SAILFISH are the prize of deep-water fishermen. The larger Pacific form commonly weighs 100 lbs.; the Atlantic form, about 60. Both are caught by trolling. Sailfish are usually released.

STRIPED MARLIN is found all year in the deep Pacific waters off the Mexican coast. It averages about 250 lbs., sometimes more than 700 lbs. It has dark vertical stripes on its sides.

TUNA are found on both coasts of Mexico, but the Skipjack and the Yellowfin are best known. Both feed on smaller fish. Yellowfins average about 100 lbs. Note finlets and yellow markings.

REPTILES are more common in Mexico than to the north, but they are neither more dangerous nor more deadly. Rattlesnakes and coral snakes occur, but not in the path of the casual visitor. In the warm lowlands are also the Fer-de-lance and the Jumping Viper. Harmless snakes are far more common. Lizards are almost everywhere. Two similar species in the northern desert are poisonous. No others can harm you despite the ferocious appearance of some. Land and water turtles are often seen. Some are hunted for food. In the coastal lowlands an alert watcher can see alligators and crocodiles.

LIZARDS are sure to be seen by visitors. Scores of small species abound. On almost every fence, bush, and tree of the Central Plateau one finds species of swifts or fence lizards. Horned lizards (1)—several species of the northern deserts and Tehuantepec —are flat-bodied insect eaters. The large, spiny iguanas (2) are vegetarian lizards that are caught for food and offered for sale in southern markets. The Common Iguana, a tree dweller, lacks the spiny tail and lives in moister regions. Finally, in the northern desert is the Beaded Lizard (3), a sluggish creature, which, with a similar close relative, are the only poisonous Mexican lizards.

SNAKES are seldom seen, unless you search for them in likely habitats. In the southern lowlands lives the Boa Constrictor (1), a harmless snake 10–12 ft. long, best known because it kills its prey by constricting. So does the Anaconda, the much larger water boa found farther south. In the same warm areas lives the Fer-de-lance (2), a 6–8-ft. pit viper with yellow markings. It is related to rattlesnakes and just as deadly. The Coral Snake (3), poisonous also, is small shy and very lightly colored.

The Tropic Racer (4), alert, rapid, and very common (3–4 ft.), feeds mainly on rodents. It is a harmless constrictor. Larger (5–8 ft.) but very similar in eating habits is the Indigo Snake (5), a snake so gentle that it can be picked up and handled with impunity. It is most common in the lowlands along both coasts. On the Central Plateau, several species of garter snakes are common in moist areas, where they feed on frogs and toads. It is a garter snake (6) that the eagle holds in Mexico's national emblem.

FRIGATE-BIRD (38 in.), or Man-O'-War, soars over both coasts, robbing gulls and terns of their catch. Note deeply forked tail and narrow wings.

CRESTED CARACARA (22 in.), a scavenger falcon, can soar like a buzzard and is seen with them. Note the crest, white throat, and pale wing tips.

BIRDS are the most difficult group to summarize in Mexico, which boasts of almost 1,000 species—more than the rest of the continent to the north. They fall into diverse groups within 89 families. Nearly 500 of these species are found only in Mexico or have ranges whose northward terminus is in Mexico. Thus over half of Mexico's birds will not be seen north of the Rio Grande. The remaining species include permanent and summer residents, whose range crosses the northern border, and a greater number of migratory species which winter in Mexico and fly north in spring to breed.

This brief sampling of about two score species excludes many common birds, such as vultures, blackbirds, nighthawks, warblers, and sparrows, that are found widely in the United States and can be identified in BIRDS OF NORTH AMERICA, a Golden Field Guide. Of the remainder, a select group of some larger, more common, or more attractive species has been illustrated.

FOR MORE ABOUT BIRDS IN MEXICO, READ:

Blake, Emmet R., BIRDS OF MEXICO. U. of Chicago Press, Chicago, 1953. The standard guide to field identification.

Sutton, G. M., MEXICAN BIRDS, First Impressions. U. of Oklahoma Press, Norman, 1951. Includes a summary of Mexican species.

Edwards, E. P., FINDING BIRDS IN MEXICO. Edwards & Co. Amherst, Va. 1968. A recently revised guide to promising areas.

ROADSIDE BIRDS are those of open country, hence likely to be seen by travelers, especially by those driving. They have little in common except for their wide distribution and preference for open areas.

COLLARED SWIFT (6 in.), one of nine Mexican species, is seen in open highland areas, flying with jerky wing-beats in search of insects. Dark males have the reddish collar, which the females lack. Similar to Chimney Swift.

VERMILLION FLYCATCHERS (5 in.), in the drier parts of Mexico, perch on acacias and other low trees and dart out after insects. The male needs no description; the gray-brown female has a streaked dull-pink breast.

MEXICAN MOTMOT (12 in.), one of six species, is locally common in dry western lowlands, south into Chiapas. Note the reddish crown and back, and the pale-blue underparts. Motmot tail feathers have a terminal tuft.

GROOVE-BILLED ANI (12 in.) is a cuckoo that looks like an overstuffed grackle. Anis travel in small flocks, feeding on insects. Often seen in bushes and thickets. The larger Smooth-billed Ani occurs on Cozumel Island.

ROADRUNNERS (22 in.) dash across roads in drier parts of Mexico, pursuing lizards and other small animals. They rarely fly. Note their slender form, long tail, and streaked underparts. A smaller species lives in the south.

61

SCARLET MACAW (36 in.) is the largest and most conspicuous parrot of Mexico, with bright colors and a long, pointed tail. It is quite common in tropical lowlands. Females are similar to males. Feeds on seeds and fruits.

ORNATE HAWK-EAGLE (24 in.) is fairly common, but not easy to see in lowland forests. It rarely soars like other hawks. Note the long, rounded tail, broad wings, and feathered feet. Feeds on small mammals and reptiles.

MONTEZUMA OROPENDOLA (20 in.) are colonial blackbirds that build many large, hanging nests. Note their pink face and orange-tipped, black bill. Females, much smaller (17 in.), do most of the nest building and care of the young.

COLLARED ARACARI (15 in.) is a lowland toucan that feeds on soft fruits. The small flocks are hard to see in the treetops. The larger, more conspicuous Sulfur-breasted Toucan may often be seen with Aracaris.

GREAT CURASSOW is a bird that looks like an overgrown, black-crested chicken. It feeds on the forest floor on insects, worms, fruits, and berries. Locally, hunted for food. Female is dull brown.

TROPICAL FOREST

BLACK-COWLED ORIOLE (8 in.) is one of ten Mexican species that make up one-third of the New World orioles. No other forest oriole has the male's rich black pattern. The female is duller, with olive on the back.

BLACK-FACED GROSBEAK (7 in.) is a bird of the treetops, where small flocks feed on fruit. The black face, bordered with bright yellow, marks the bird, which is otherwise yellowish to gray. Female similar to male.

RUFOUS-TAILED JACAMAR (10 in.) perches on branches in dense woods and darts after insects. Note the long, slender bill. Female similar to male, but with a buff throat. Jacamars nest in burrows 1–2 ft. deep dug in earth or sand.

RED-CAPPED MANAKIN (4 in.) is quite common in the forest understory. The male is unmistakable; female dull olive. Manakins feed on berries and insects. When courting, males make a loud buzzing noise with their wings.

GRAY-NECKED WOOD RAIL (15 in.) is a bird of coastal lowlands and mangrove swamps. It is not easy to see but is not as elusive as other rails. This narrow-bodied, weak flier stalks small aquatic animals in the marsh grasses.

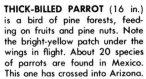

THICK-BILLED PARROT (16 in.) is a bird of pine forests, feeding on fruits and pine nuts. Note the bright-yellow patch under the wings in flight. About 20 species of parrots are found in Mexico. This one has crossed into Arizona.

GRAY SILKY FLYCATCHER (8 in.) represents a small family related to waxwings. Feeds on mistletoe berries, other fruits, and insects. The crest and white tail patch are good field marks. Females browner than males.

MOUNTAIN TROGON (12 in.), with a long tail, is typical of oak forests. Feeds on insects and fruit. Nests in holes in trees. Eight species of trogons live in Mexico, including the famous and rare Quetzal of southern mountains.

BROWN-BACKED SOLITAIRE (8 in.), a woodland thrush, is often captured and kept as a cage-bird because of its fine song of clear, bell-like notes. In the field, look for the gray head, white eye ring, olive-brown back.

AZTEC THRUSH (8½ in.) is found only in the high mountains. Note the white on the belly, wings, and tail. Female is like the male, but paler and more streaked with buff. About two dozen species of thrushes live in Mexico.

HOODED GROSBEAK (7 in.) is a seed-eating species that may descend to the lowlands in winter. Similar to northern grosbeaks, this one has a distinctly black head, wings, and tail. Female is duller—brownish, with less black.

BLUE-HOODED EUPHONIA (4½ in.) is a tanager—one of 24 species found from Mexico south. Note small size, short tail, and brilliant colors of male. Female is olive green. Feeds on mistletoe berries; builds a domed nest.

BLACK-HEADED SISKIN (5 in.), a finch, with black head and splash of yellow on the black wing. Note heavy bill and notched tail. These seed-eaters of pine and oak woods have an undulating flight. Females resemble males.

RED-FACED WARBLER (5 in.) does cross the Rio Grande a bit, but ten other warblers never get north of Mexico. The Red-faced is an insect-eating bird of pine forests. Note red face and breast on both male and female.

MEXICAN JUNCO (6 in.) may be seen in small flocks in most mountain areas, hunting seeds on the ground. Male and female are alike. Note chestnut back, gray breast and belly, and black at base of bill.

65

SNAIL KITE (19 in.) is the same species that barely survives in the Florida Everglades. Here it is more common in Atlantic lowland marshes. Note the black body, white-tipped tail, and slender, curved bill.

BLACK-THROATED ORIOLE (10 in.) is a large species found in eastern lowlands to Central America. Note its large size, its white wing bar, and yellow wing patch. Female duller and more gray.

FORK-TAILED FLYCATCHER (15 in.) has a very long tail. Do not confuse with the slightly smaller Scissor-tailed Flycatcher (a migrant) that lacks black on its gray head. The Fork-tailed is found only in the lowlands.

AMERICAN JACANA (9 in.), with very long toes, walks easily on floating water plants. No other bird can be confused with this spectacular wader. Male and female are similar; the young are a dull gray-brown.

RUFESCENT TINAMOU (11 in.), the most common of four Mexican species, is a primitive bird that searches thickets for fruits and seeds. Note buff bars on wings. Its clear whistle is often heard, but the bird is hard to see.

PACIFIC LOWLANDS

ORANGE-FRONTED PARAKEET
(9 in.) is common along the Pacific, from Durango south. Flocks feed on fruit and seeds. Note the orange forehead and blue on the wings. The similar Green Parakeet lacks this blue.

WHITE-FRONTED PARROT (10 in.) is a short-tailed bird of the dry Pacific lowlands. Note the white forehead, blue spot on the crown, and the red wing patch which the females lack. This parrot talks well and makes a good pet.

YELLOW-WINGED CACIQUE (12 in.) is a large. crested blackbird. No other bird has this yellow-and-black pattern. Female smaller and duller. Colonial flocks build clusters of hanging nests.

MAGPIE JAY (24 in.), with a 15-in. tail and a blue crest, has variable amounts of black on the head and throat. Males and females identical. Abundant and unmistakable, as are its loud calls and whistles.

ORANGE-BREASTED BUNTING (5 in.), found only in dry Pacific lowlands, is a colorful bird with a bright-green crown. Ranks with the Painted Bunting as the most colorful finches. Female similar, but duller.

male female

Black-crested Coquette

Violet-crowned Hummer

Fork Tailed Emerald

Berylline Hummer

Long-tailed Hermit

Long-billed Star Throat

HUMMINGBIRDS

BLACK-CRESTED COQUETTE (2½ in.) is the smallest of all Mexican hummers. It has a spotted abdomen and a sparkling green crown and crest. Female similar, but lacks the crest.

FORK-TAILED EMERALD (3 in.), of central and southern Mexico, has a deeply forked, blue-black tail. Male is a rich metallic green; female grayer. All hummers lay two tiny white eggs.

LONG-BILLED STAR THROAT (5 in.), a hummer of lowland coastal forests, has a metallic-green crown and a red throat patch. Female similar to male, duller, without throat patch.

VIOLET-CROWNED HUMMER (4 in.) is found only in western and south-central Mexico. The only species in its range with completely white underparts. Female similar to male.

BERYLLINE HUMMER (4 in.), a very abundant species, is found almost everywhere, except on the highest mountains. Note the purple and warm brown on the wings and tail.

LONG-TAILED HERMIT (6 in.), of tropical lowlands, is unique among Mexico's 60 species of hummingbirds. Note the very long curved bill and the tail with white-tipped feathers.

MAMMALS include many species whose range extend north into the U.S.: opossums, bats, raccoons, otters, skunks, foxes, wolves, beaver, squirrels, porcupines, bears, rabbits, deer, and many others. But in Mexico's tropical areas are other mammals whose ranges scarcely reach the central highland. These pages sample the mammals that never or hardly ever reach the southern boundary of the U.S. The larger mammals are now rare and may be seen only in wilderness areas.

FOR MORE ABOUT MEXICAN MAMMALS, READ:

Leopold, A. Starker, WILDLIFE OF MEXICO. U. of California Press, Berkeley, 1959. A complete study of game birds and mammals; rich bibliography of English and Spanish titles.

Villa, Bernardo R., WILD MAMMALS OF THE VALLEY OF MEXICO. Annals of the Inst. of Biology, U. of Mexico, Vol. 23, No. 1–2, Mexico, D.F., 1952. A detailed survey—in Spanish.

Zim, H.S. and Donald Hoffmeister, MAMMALS. Golden Press, New York, 1955. Refer to species with ranges extending southward.

RINGTAILS (2 species) and the animals below are all in the raccoon family. Ringtails are smaller than raccoons, with conspicuously ringed tail. Found in dry, wooded areas. Length: 30 in.

COATI is raccoon-size, but more slender, with a longer snout and tail, often held upright. Feeds on fruits, berries, and insects, in tropical forests and coastal plains. Length: 40 in.

KINKAJOU, rarest and most nocturnal of the raccoons, has a flat face, large eyes, small ears, and a long, monkey-like tail. Lives in southern forests; feeds on fruits and small animals. Length: 36 in.

69

Collared Peccary

White-lipped Peccary

PECCARIES (2 species) are small wild pigs weighing up to 50 lbs. The more common has a light "collar." The rarer southern species has a white face. Both feed in small bands, on nuts, fruits, roots, and soft plants. Widely hunted for food and hides.

TAPIR, a distant relative of the horse, is now rare in the rain forests. It prefers swamps and stays in water much of the time, feeding on succulent plants. Young have light bands; adults a long, trunklike nose. Weight: about 500 lbs.

ANTEATERS are tree-dwelling, primitive rain-forest mammals. One squirrel-sized species is orange-brown and very rare. The larger, dog-sized Collared Anteater has a long snout and tail and large claws. Tears open ant and termite nests for food.

NINE-BANDED ARMADILLO lives in burrows, except in deserts. Feeds at night, largely on insects. These odd, almost toothless mammals are protected by an armored skin. They are hunted for their sweet, tasty flesh. Length: 30 in.

JAGUAR (*el tigre*) is the big cat of Mexico—over 7 ft. long, weight up to 250 lbs. Note its spots in rosettes. Larger than the Puma (which is more common), the Jaguar lives in forests and in coastal lowlands. Hunts only at night.

JAGUARUNDI is a medium-sized (3½–4 ft.), tawny cat, like a small Puma. Some are reddish-brown; some nearly black. Hunts on the ground for rodents, rabbits, and birds, but will hide in trees when hunted. Usually two young to a litter.

OCELOT is about half a Jaguar's length, but only about one-tenth its weight. The fur is spotted and streaked, never in rosettes. This is the only common, medium-sized, spotted cat. Ocelots also hunt at night. Range like that of Jaguar.

MARGAY is about the size of a Bobcat (2–3 ft.), which is also common in Mexico. It is spotted like the Ocelot with black or dark brown. The two are hard to tell apart. Margays are very rare and not often seen. Prefer hunting in trees for small mammals.

HOWLERS are large, (33 in.) heavy-bodied monkeys whose roaring cries echo in rain and cloud forests. Fur is reddish-brown or black, and males have a long "beard." Bands travel in treetops, feeding on fruits. Females have one baby, which they carry.

SPIDER MONKEYS, smaller (18 in.), more slender, and with very long arms, are more common and have a wider range. Bands of a dozen or more live and feed together in their own territory. They resemble Howlers in feeding habits. Both hunted for food.

PACAS are large (26 in.) rodents of tropical forests and openings. They live in underground dens and feed at night, entirely on plants. Hunted for their fine-tasting meat and for their skins.

AGOUTIS are smaller (20 in.) than Pacas and closely related. Two color phases exist—black and brown—often in separate areas. May feed by day when not disturbed, otherwise by night.

Manatee (Sea Cow)

California Sea Lion

Harbor Porpoise

MARINE MAMMALS are not easy to see but are all the more exciting when they appear. In coves and protected areas of both the Gulf of Mexico and the Gulf of California lives the Manatee (Sea Cow), which feeds on water plants. Its front legs are flippers. It has no hind legs but uses its broad, flat tail in swimming.

The Pacific waters have a greater variety of marine mammals. Rarest and most interesting are the large Elephant Seals, found only on Guadalupe Island,

west of Baja California Sur. But more likely to be seen are the California Sea Lions, large western seals that hunt fish along the rocky coasts. This species is the "trained seal" of the circuses.

Farther out at sea, Harbor Porpoises, small toothed whales, often race along the bows of ships. But most interesting of all are the great Gray Whales (40 ft.), which migrate down the Pacific coast in spring to breed in the waters of the Scammon Lagoon of Baja California.

Gray Whale

CULTURES OF EARLY MEXICO

Mexico's story began over 20,000 years ago as descendants of migrants who had crossed from Asia to Alaska, some 10–25,000 years earlier, reached the upland valleys. As shown above, these primitive hunters even fought the great mammoth. From Tlopacoya comes an obsidian knife possibly 24,000 years old. At Tepexpan, a skeleton, dated about 12,000 B.C., was found with mammoth bones and projectile points. From these beginnings developed the many cultures that can be studied at the archeological sites for which Mexico is famous.

MEXICO IN 1519 The Aztec Empire (yellow), after some 200 years of wars and conquests, now included semi-independent states (purple). Unconquered states are in red. To the north were independent farming tribes (green) and hunting tribes (brown).

Hunters at Tepexpan attack a mammoth.

These archeological sites were occupied at overlapping periods from about 600 B.C. to 1525. Some of the richest sites are listed below and are located on the map at the left, by number.

When the Spanish came in 1519, they conquered most of central Mexico and absorbed or subjugated the local tribes. The Maya centers in Yucatan had already begun to decline. The dry northern areas were occupied by small, often impoverished groups of farmers and hunters.

1. Calixtlahuaca, Toluca, Mexico, Toltec and Aztec, 300 B.C.–1500.
2. Chichen-Itza, Yucatan, Maya and Toltec, 300–1400. Cenote. (p. 89)
3. Cholula, Puebla, Archaic to Aztec, 500 B.C.–1525. Large pyramid.
4. Kabah, Yucatan, Maya, 10th century. Ornamented pyramid. (p. 89)
5. Malinalco, Mexico, Aztec, 1476–1525. Temple of Warriors.
6. Mitla, Oaxaca, Mixtec, 900–1521. (p. 85)
7. Monte Alban, Oaxaca, Zapotec, 700 B.C.–900. Fine architecture.
8. Palenque, Chiapas, Maya, 200–900. By air or rail only. (p. 87)
9. Sayil, Yucatan, Maya, 800–900. Simple geometric decoration.
10. Tajin, Veracruz, Totonac, 300–900. Pyramid with niches. (p. 83)
11. Tenayuca, Mexico, Chichimec, 1100–1525. Pyramid.
12. Tenochtitlan, Mexico City, Aztec, 1325–1520. Aztec Capital. (p. 94)
13. Teotihuacan, Mexico, Classic, 400 B.C.–650. Great Pyramids. (p. 80)
14. Tula, Hidalgo, Toltec, 11th and 12th centuries. Toltec Capital. (p. 90)
15. Tulum, Queretaro, Maya, 10th century. Ornate frescoes. (p. 89)
16. Tzintzuntzan, Michoacan, Tarascan, 900–1525. Temples.
17. Uxmal, Yucatan, Maya, 10th century. Grotesque mosaics. (p. 89)
18. Xochicalco, Morelos, 300–900. A city and fort. (p. 83)

MEXICO'S GROWTH began with the permanent settlements made possible by agriculture which got under way about 6000 B.C. Soon farming was well established as the basic way of life. Little is known of the people who farmed until about 2000 B.C., when new and distinct cultures began to emerge in the small lake-dotted depression later known as the Valley of Mexico and elsewhere. Farming was not easy in the semi-arid climate, so it is not surprising that the first gods were rain gods.

PEOPLE were now full-fledged farmers who lived in villages of adobe huts or houses of woven sticks covered with mud (wattle). By now, too, corn, beans, and squash had become the Mexican trinity. These farmers also had avocados, tomatoes, fruits, and herbs. They grew cotton and wove maguey fiber. Burials, dated about 500 B.C., yielded fine ceramics, bone and stone ornaments, figurines, and baskets. In the previous millenium or two, new cultural trends had been clearly established.

CORN (maize) was gathered as early as 4000 B.C. Later this wild plant with acorn-sized ears was domesticated. It crossed with

From about 300 B.C. to 900 A.D., ancient Mexico reckoned its golden age. Great religious and cultural centers arose. Monuments and inscriptions give a calendar and a record of important events. Most of the great archeological sites (p. 74) developed in this period. By 900 A.D., invading nomads from the north had come in several waves, destroying much of the old or adapting it into their own culture. Last came the Aztecs, who founded their capital—a scarce 200 years before Cortes.

similar grasses, and by 900 B.C. farmers grew corn with thumb-sized ears. Corn soon became the basic food of the Mexicans.

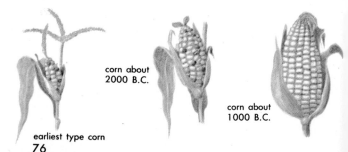

corn about
2000 B.C.

corn about
1000 B.C.

earliest type corn

Pyramid at Cuicuilco, near Mexico City.

CUICUILCO is an archaic "pyramid" located in the Pedregal, south of Mexico City. Dated between 500 and 100 B.C., some claim it is the oldest structure in the New World. The lava flow from the Xitle volcano partly buried the site about 2,000 years ago. Excavations disclose the "pyramid" has a diameter of 420 feet and its abutments align due east-west. Several altars have been uncovered and various artifacts found. Tunnels show several additions to the original mound.

COPILCO, dated 900–500 B.C., is a burial site near Cuicuilco. Here, under lava 30 ft. thick, are 3 skeletons, identical with those of modern Mexicans, and many pieces of ceramics and stonework. This site is more evidence of an established population in the valley around Mexico City at an early date, with advanced and distinctive pottery and characteristic figurines (below left).

TLATILCO, west of Mexico City, flourished at the same time as Copilco, though it probably began much earlier. Found here are a large number of realistic figurines in great variety (below right), giving a rare insight into these early times. Skeletons at Tlatilco show trepanning (skull surgery) with some healing, which proves survival and indicates rare medical skill.

Ceramics from ancient burials in the Valley of Mexico.

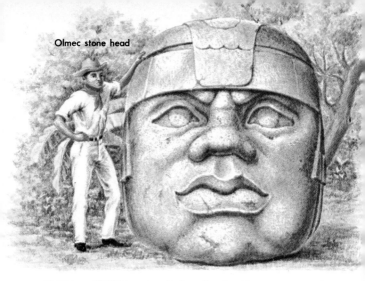

Olmec stone head

OLMEC CULTURE flourished early (1200–150 B.C.) in the warm Gulf lowlands. Little is known about these people, but statues show them with long heads and receding foreheads that were flattened in infancy. They filed their teeth and perforated their nose and ear lobes to hold ornaments.

Huge heads with feline and Negroid features were carved from volcanic rock that was hauled at least 60 miles. The Olmec were also excellent potters and carvers of jade who developed hieroglyphics (picture symbols of dates and events) and also a calendar. The earliest inscription deciphered is Sept. 2, 31 B.C. But Olmec temples, built of wood and thatch, have perished.

The tiger was worshiped as their god of rain and fertility who "lived in the heart of the earth." Olmec influence in art and religion extended north to Tlatilco (p. 77); later into Teotihuacan (p. 80); into Guerrero and throughout the lands of the Mayas.

Olmec ceramics, Veracruz

A SYSTEM OF COUNTING set on the base 20 (vigesimal) was an early Olmec contribution. The system is just as logical as our system with the base 10. The Mayas developed this system further and adapted the concept of zero—a Toltec invention. Both the Olmecs and the Mayas wrote numbers with a series of dots and bars as illustrated for the Mayas below. The Aztecs used dots up to 19, and for 20 and its multiples, used other signs.

The counting system made use of position to show values of 20 and its multiples, as our decimal shows values of ten. A second method of writing numbers, often seen on stelae, uses the heads of gods for numbers from 1 to 13.

Two calendars served the ancient Mexicans, who had also a fine knowledge of astronomy. In the ceremonial year 20 days were repeated 13 times for a total of 260. Each day was designated by a name plus a number as 2 *Cib* or 5 *Kan*.

The civil (solar) year had 18 months of 20 days, plus a closing period of 5 evil days for a 365-day year. The civil and ceremonial years were intricately related. Every 52 civil years and 73 ceremonial years, the calendars began on the same New Year's Day. This period of 18,980 days or 52 years became a sacred cycle. The Aztecs believed the world ended with each cycle, unless the gods acted. They watched all night. At sunrise, the sacred fire rekindled, life began anew.

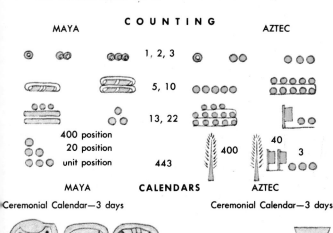

COUNTING

MAYA　　　　　　　　　　　　AZTEC

1, 2, 3		
5, 10		
13, 22		

400 position
20 position
unit position
443

400　　40　3

CALENDARS

MAYA　　　　　　　　　　　AZTEC

Ceremonial Calendar—3 days　　　　Ceremonial Calendar—3 days

Imix　　Cimi　　Chuen　　　Cipatli　　Ehecatl　　Calli

Pyramid of the Moon

TEOTIHUACAN is a Nahuatl (p. 114) name meaning "where the ancient gods lived," for the pyramids here were built long ago by ancient people who, one expert believes, migrated west from the Gulf. Anyhow, the Teotihuacan people were farmers who worshiped the life-giving sun and rain gods.

This great religious complex, with its long Avenue of the Dead (the names are all modern), covers an area of some 2,000 acres.

PYRAMID OF THE SUN (base 690 ft.; height, 210) is the largest structure, 20 stories high; originally of earth; later covered with rock. Its simple plan, without embellishments, shows technical skill, and orientation with seasonal movements of the sun. One estimate: it took 10,000 workers 20 years to build.

PYRAMID OF THE MOON, older and smaller (140 ft. high) than the Pyramid of the Sun, stands at the end of the Avenue of the Dead, which was a main avenue to the pyramids and to the many temples above and around them. Nearby were homes of priests and nobles and, farther off, less pretentious houses. Frescoes, pottery, jade, and stonework attest to the artistic skill of the inhabitants.

The priests, who were also mathematicians, astronomers, and philosophers, interpreted the world and the gods to the people, assembled at ceremonies. The area prospered with peace and good crops. It was maintained and developed until the 7th century, when hordes of nomadic hunters began invading from the north, burning and destroying much of Teotihuacan, which by 1000 was abandoned.

Pottery and beads from Teotihuacan.

TLALOC, God of Rain, (above) was one of the most important gods at Teotihuacan. A fine mural of Tlaloc (below) was found on walls near the Pyramid of the Sun—perhaps in a priest's dwelling. Tlaloc is shown rising from the waves and bringing water to the people. He is surrounded by marine animals and shells.

Some 150 murals have been uncovered recently at Teotihuacan. Other ornaments show that bright earth colors were widely used and that the temple areas were gay and attractive.

Arts at peaceful Teotihuacan developed through the centuries. Their stone masks with delicate features were traded to distant places. They made pottery of several types, including dishes, bowls, and highly ornamented polychromes; also many kinds of figurines.

QUETZALCOATL, the Feathered Serpent, (above) held second place to Tlaloc, but gradually he became the major god. His ornate temple, with polychrome heads, was built much later than the great pyramids.

Later, with the Toltec and the Aztec, Quetzalcoatl took the highest place among the gods. Temples to Quetzalcoatl are found throughout central Mexico. He became the all-powerful God of Life, creator of gods as well as men. Quetzalcoatl is shown in many forms, often with two faces, as he was God of both the morning and evening stars. People drew blood from their ears and tongue to mix with copal (incense) as self-sacrifice offerings to him. Many incense burners have been found. Later, under the Aztecs, thousands of prisoners were sacrificed.

PACIFIC COAST CULTURES also had early beginnings, perhaps even before 1200 B.C. Between 200 B.C. and 800 A.D., great ceremonial centers were built by these hunters, fishermen, and farmers. The centers, dedicated to gods of fire, rain, and fertility, lacked large pyramids, temples, and monuments. As many as 20 separate areas may be involved. All had a common denominator of handsome, realistic pottery and figures, free of religious connotations. After 800 A.D. these centers declined. Tarascans from Michoacan entered the area with copper tools and superior weapons. Later, the centers were abandoned, but typical pottery continued till about 1500.

Nayarit musician

Colima pumpkin pot

Colima dogs

WESTERN POTTERY, mainly from Nayarit, Jalisco, and Colima exhibits a variety of styles. Colima has simple hollow figures of warriors, ballplayers, musicians, and women carrying children or burdens. Many animals were made, especially the fattened dogs sold for food in the marketplaces. Nayarit figures, some large and often with a cream slip, show similar subjects, including family groups, but in a different style.

NEW CULTURES were flourishing to the east by 300 A.D.—Tajin, Cholula, Xochicalco, and Zapotec. The great Mayan religious centers also date from this time. Teotihuacan, too, underwent a great revival. The period from 300 to about 900 was a propitious one.

TAJIN is now a large ruin hidden in the coastal jungle near Papantla. Its culture may have come from the Olmecs or from Teotihuacan. Here were found palm-shaped carvings, stone yokes, and other delicate and refined sculpture. Its seven-story pyramid has unusual window-like panels, as decor.

XOCHICALCO, south of Cuernavaca is a large center and fort, begun about 300. Here are lavish temples to Quetzalcoatl (with some Mayan influence) and wall reliefs—recalling a meeting in the year 600 to reconcile differences in calendars. Here, too, may be the oldest ball court. Teams competed to get the rubber ball through a stone ring set high in the wall—with players using only legs, elbows, and hips.

CHOLULA, near Puebla (300–1200), is the site of the world's largest pyramid, with a base of over 40 acres. Begun by Teotihuanecans, it consists of seven superimposed structures. Later, the Toltecs set up the worship of Quetzalcoatl, and Cholula became a ceremonial center. Cholula maintained its temples until the Conquest. Recent excavations reveal an even greater Cholula than previously known.

Cholula polychrome pottery

Xochicalco pottery

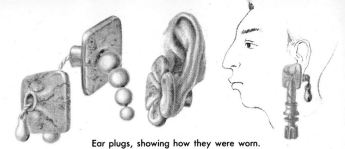

Ear plugs, showing how they were worn.

THE ZAPOTECS, who entered the Valley of Oaxaca about 300, found a remarkable religious complex of temples and burials on a mountaintop above the present city of Oaxaca. We know very little of the people who built this Monte Alban complex. They may have entered the valley between 700–300 B.C. and, at this period, built the First Temple with its famous reliefs of dancers—figures (pictured below) that show Olmec influence.

Another wave of settlers, possibly from Guatemala, came about 300 B.C. They built a massive observatory, erected huge stone columns, and made pots with four legs. Within 300 years or so this culture disappeared.

With the Zapotecs began the flowering of Monte Alban. From 300–1000 they restored the mountaintop, adding great platforms, temples, and a ball court. Their majestic, simple architecture made Monte Alban spectacular. All the arts flourished. Noteworthy are the large, ornate funerary urns.

By the 10th century, building ceased. Other cities in the valley became important, and Monte Alban was used only for burials—by Zapotecs and later by Mixtecs. The Mixtecs fought with the Zapotecs, when they first came into the valley, but later they allied against the Aztecs, who penetrated the area and established military outposts.

Mixtec gold and polychrome pottery—Oaxaca.

THE MIXTECS, who lived northwest of the Zapotecs, were pushed out of their lands, around 1200, by Chichimecs. They moved south into the Valley of Oaxaca—perhaps even farther. The Mixtecs established several centers in and around Oaxaca. Of these sites, Mitla, some 25 miles south of Oaxaca, is best known. This site was occupied since very early times, but its big development, as a place of burial for nobility, did not take place until after the decline of Monte Alban (p. 84), which was still used as a burial site at about the year 1200. Its famous tomb No. 7 yielded over 500 pieces of Mixtecan treasure, including exquisite goldwork, jade, carved bone, and polychrome pottery, now seen in the museum at Oaxaca.

At Mitla, a series of buildings were made of rock and mud, covered below with rock slabs and above with intricate stone mosaics, meticulously cut and fitted into over 20 different meandering designs (below). The mosaics for the Building of Columns took about 100,000 pieces. The Mixtecs were not architects like the Zapotecs; they were craftsmen, who developed pieces of great beauty and fine detail. Not far from Mitla is the center of Yagul, a fortress city with temples and palaces that have been partly restored. The age of Yagul is about the same as Mitla.

THE MAYAS,

dating back to at least 500 B.C., differ from people of the Valley of Mexico in appearance and language. Within this linguistic family are a number of groups. All but one are contiguous in southern Mexico and Central America. During a long formative period, the Mayan farmers made simple pottery and built low platforms for their temples and houses. After 300, priests developed a knowledge of astronomy, mathematics, and hieroglyphics. They supervised the building of great religious centers, where the arts flourished. Yet, about 800, for causes still unknown, the great monuments were destroyed and the temples abandoned.

MAYAN FARMERS made clearings in the forest to plant their corn. After a few years they left the worn, leached soil and made new clearings, where they also grew beans, peppers, tomatoes, vanilla, and fruits like papaya and zapote. The turkey was domesticated; bees were kept for honey. Game and fish added protein to their diet. Mayas worked wood and stone skillfully without use of metal tools. They grew fibers for clothing, mats, and baskets; and made pottery and worked copper and gold.

THE DISSOLUTION of the classic Mayan centers is still a mystery. Soil depletion or civil unrest may have been a cause. As the inland centers were abandoned, new centers began in Yucatan. These rose between 1000 and 1200; earlier ones showing Toltec influence. Three of the centers (Uxmal, Mayapan, and Chichen-Itza) later formed an alliance, but social deterioration set in again. When the Spanish came to Yucatan, the cities were empty, and the people had dispersed.

Palenque temple and tower

PALENQUE, the most impressive of the Mayan ceremonial cities, was set in the humid, wooded foothills about 60 miles from Villahermosa. Here, half a dozen large temples and many smaller ones were built. The main ones were steeply stepped and were topped by a two-chambered building. The temples are close together, though the inhabited area may have extended 3 to 5 miles. In addition to the temples and a ball court, there is a large complex of buildings—a palace with a four-story tower, several patios, many rooms and galleries.

Best known of the buildings is the Temple of the Inscriptions which bears many glyphs. These seem to date the temple at 692.

When this building was studied in 1949 by the Mexican archeologist Albert Ruz, he noticed that one floor slab moved. Beneath was a stairway choked with rubbled. Cleaned out, it led to a crypt with a sarcophagus containing the skeleton of a nobleman or priest, bedecked with jade and other jewels. This great treasure and a model of the tomb can be seen at the Museum of Anthropology.

| Ceramic head | Jade mask | Cross of Palenque |

murals—Bonampak

murals—North wall

BONAMPAK is now an isolated ruin, deep in Chiapas near the Guatemalan border. It lies in the Usumacinta River drainage, where two other great Mayan centers were located. Bonampak was never completely abandoned. The Lacandones, Mayas of Chiapas, still go there to burn incense in the overgrown ruins.

While photographing the Lacandones in 1946, Giles G. Healey gained their confidence and was taken by them to Bonampak. He was the first outsider to see the eight white-walled temples that mark the ruins. In the plaza is a massive stela and many more that were broken and half buried. Here, too, were stucco figures of jaguars and serpents—amid vines and trees, ruin and rubble.

Healey's exploration took him into a dark, narrow, vaulted chamber completely covered with murals. Two other chambers shared this richness, portraying priests, warriors, nobles, musicians, dancers, and battle scenes. Experts have copied the murals, which can now be seen in Mexico City, but Bonampak has yet to be restored. The name is Mayan for "painted walls."

Experts believe Bonampak was an offshoot of the larger center of Yaxchilan on the Usumacinta River. This, too, has barely been touched. Farther down the river, and on the Guatemalan side, is Piedras Negras, the third of these Mayan centers. Well-preserved but broken stelae here have dated the occupancy. All were at their prime about the year 700—the golden age of the Mayas.

THE MAYAS OF YUCATAN also built religious centers as they began to settle on the Peninsula. Mayas from the interior joined them as they abandoned their own religious centers after 800.

Yucatan is largely semiarid, and rain is quickly absorbed by the soft lime rock. Occasionally the rock caves in, making the underground water available in *cenotes*, or natural wells. The Mayas found these *cenotes* and settled around them. Under Toltec direction (pp. 90–91), they began to build temples at Chichen-Itza, Kabah, Labna, Uxmal, and Tulum. Toltec influence is seen best in Chichen-Itza. Itza is the Mayan name for the Toltec, and Chichen-Itza means "the Toltec place at the well."

Castillo at Chichen-Itza

Here the largest Yucatan complex was built around a temple to the God Kukulcan—the Mayan name for Quetzalcoatl, the Toltec God. Other aspects of Chichen-Itza, as the jaguars, serpents, skulls, and the reclining, rain-giving Chacmools, are also of Toltec origin. One of the two *cenotes* became a sacrificial well, into which valuable offerings were thrown, as well as captives, maidens, and children, all gifts to the Rain God.

Sacred Well at Chichen-Itza

Jaguar Throne, Chichen-Itza

Other Mayan centers in Yucatan have features worth seeing. Tulum, near Cozumel Island, has a temple with frescoes. At Uxmal is a large pyramid, the ornate Palace of the Governors, and buildings decorated with masks of the Rain God, Chac. At Kabah, the coiled tongue of Chac forms a step at the Codz-Pop. His hooked nose decorates this temple's facade.

89

Toltec pyramid at Tula with Atlantes statues

THE TOLTECS were nomads of Chichimec stock who began to invade the Valley of Mexico in the 8th century. After destroying many religious centers, the Toltecs (reed people), later united under Chief Mixcoatl, settled down and began to farm. Still later, under their King Quetzalcoatl (son of Mixcoatl), who took on the name of the God (p. 81), a new capital was built at Tula, about 50 miles north of Mexico City. This became a trading center and the site of a great pyramid with many Atlantes figures. Here the Toltecs prospered, developing irrigation, metallurgy, architecture, arts and crafts.

The remains of Tula, unearthed and restored, show that the Toltec legends did not exaggerate the splendor of their capital. Its many temples and magnificent palaces were once decorated with gold, shells, turquoise, and feathers. On market day, the central plaza overflowed with people trading cloth, feathers, skins, pottery and food.

TOLTEC RELIGION was the worship of Quetzalcoatl. However, factions developed; favoring human sacrifices and those opposed. Finally, King Quetzalcoatl (who opposed) was forced to flee from Tula. With followers, he went to Cholula (p. 83), in 999, and there remained after rebuilding the temple to Quetzalcoatl. After some 20 years, he went on to Yucatan, where his influence is seen in the buildings at Chichen-Itza (p. 89). The legend of his promised return helped pave the way for Cortes in 1519.

Quetzalcoatl—carving

ARTS AND CRAFTS reached high levels at Tula. The potters were excellent, noted for their censers, used in ceremonies. Cotton was grown, dyed, and made into bright clothing. Maguey was planted and used as a fiber. Pulque was first made from it here. The nobles wore feathered headdresses and elaborate clothing ornamented with gold. Jewelry of jade and turquoise, silver and obsidian has been found. Of all the arts, sculpture was outstanding, as columns, figures, and reliefs on many buildings.

Toltec pottery

THE DECLINE of Toltec rule began about 1150, because of inner conflict and lack of a unifying leader. A series of revolutions broke out, possibly connected with foreign segments of the population. King Huemac fled in 1168 and during the next 50 years his empire fell apart and was taken over by northern invaders (also Chichimec tribes), just as the Toltecs took over the area some 300 years earlier.

Toltec Chacmool, a rain-deity.

Huitzilopochtli
(Sun God)

THE AZTECS, last of the nomadic Chichimec invaders from the north, pushed into the Valley of Mexico around 1200. They were looking for a permanent home—a land promised them by their Sun God, Huitzilopochtli. Within a century and a half—through conquest and alliances—the Aztecs became masters of Mexico, receiving enormous tribute and large conscript armies.

WANDERING for well over two centuries made the Aztecs a poor but hardy lot when they reached the Valley of Mexico. They had few possessions outside their clothing, tools, and weapons, but they were skilled warriors and inured to hardships. The tribe traveled under the leadership of four chieftain-priests who carried their stone Sun God (above).

Four times prior to reaching the Valley of Mexico, the Aztecs had stopped to observe the end of a 52-year solar cycle. The Aztecs were permitted to settle on a rocky and swampy island in Lake Texcoco, now part of Mexico City. Here they found all the good omens—white plants, a twin spring flowing red and blue water, and, finally, an eagle grasping a snake, perched on a cactus. Here the Aztecs built their capital, Tenochtitlan.

The Aztecs began in a small way. They fished and hunted. The surplus was traded for stone and wood for their homes and temples. Hired out as mercenaries to the local kings, the Aztecs shifted their loyalty with circumstances and soon conquered the surrounding tribes. They permitted the conquered people to govern themselves, but extracted tribute and conscripted soldiers. Aztec power and wealth grew and by 1450 much of central Mexico was under their control.

Aztec migrations, from Bolurina Codex

THE DOMINANT AZTECS strengthened every phase of their government. They provided a strict education for all boys and an even more rigorous program for sons of nobles or boys of high intelligence, who might become rulers or priests.

The priesthood was increased, and ceremonials became major social events. These included a great number of human sacrifices. Priests knew the calendar and set dates for planting, harvesting, and ceremonies. The Aztec "calendar stone" (right) carved in 1469 is not a calendar at all; it honors the sun and shows four 52-year cycles. See it at the Museum of Anthropology.

Aztec "Calendar" Stone; three feet thick, twelve feet in diameter; shows four 52 year cycles.

As the Aztecs advanced, their social structure became more complex and a class system separated nobles from commoners. The Aztec ruler was first elected; later the throne supposedly passed from brother to brother and, when no brothers were left, to the oldest son of the first brother. Montezuma's headdress of quetzal feathers and gold (right) is a fine example of the elegance of royal dress. The original is in Vienna; the one at the Nat. Museum of Anthropology is a copy.

Montezuma's headdress; made of approximately 400 green quetzal feathers and gold.

The Aztec culture, geared to warfare, had to expand continually and to acquire a broader base. Thousands of captives were needed for religious sacrifices. The support of nobles and priests demanded increased tribute. The stone of Tizoc (right) was carved to commemorate Aztec victories. Details show the Aztec conquest of Tuxpan (Place of the Rabbit) and other sites.

Stone of Tizac records Aztec victories; can be seen at Museum of Anthropology in Mexico City.

Restoration of Tenochtitlan at the time of the conquest—
a mural at the National Museum of Anthropology.

TENOCHTITLAN, the capital (now downtown Mexico City), was the pride of all Aztecs. Each of the nine kings (from 1376–1520) added to its splendor. The city was both the nation's capital and its ''shining religious center.'' To the Aztecs, church and state were one and the same —inseparable.

In Aztec belief, all knowledge and skill (even that of pulque making) was a gift of the gods to their chosen people. In return, the Aztecs built many temples to their many gods and goddesses. Major ceremonies sought rain from Tlaloc and offered blood to Huitzilopochtli, so he could fight the powers of darkness. Human sacrifices were also made to Quetzalcoatl and other gods.

Dominating Tenochtitlan's main plaza was a great pyramid topped by twin temples to the sun and rain gods. Flanking this, were temples to Quetzalcoatl and his dark twin, Tezcatlipoca. Near the plaza were some 70 other temples, ball courts, palaces for the king and his extended family, and for noblemen and priests; also, buildings for the royal zoo and botanical garden. Warehouses bulged with tribute; racks of skulls and piles of human bones attested to the people's devotion to the gods.

By the time of the Conquest, Tenochtitlan was a city of 60,000 houses and 300,000 people, connected to the mainland by five wide causeways. An aqueduct brought fresh water from Chapultepec. The markets were crowded with people and goods, brought by canoe and on the backs of carriers. Much of this great city was destroyed in the Conquest. Its stones were used in Spanish buildings till all of Tenochtitlan disappeared. Later excavations disclosed remains, now seen at the N.E. corner of the Zocalo.

CODICES are hand-painted "books" of pictures, counts, and glyphs. Thousands were made before the Spanish Conquest; a few after. Some were tax and tribute records; others told of the gods, prophecies, ceremonies, and traditions. The few codices that remain are treasured in great libraries. See the examples above and below.

MOST CODICES were made of the pounded inner bark of wild fig trees, bonded with gum and covered with lime. This gave the paper a durable, parchment-like finish. The priest or scribe usually outlined the pictures or glyphs in dark lines and later filled in color, using vegetable, animal, and mineral paints that are still bright after centuries. A codex was folded like an accordion and bound between two covers of wood and leather. Codices varied in size. One famous codex is 23 ft. long and 9 in. wide. It folds 5 in. thick and has a total of 112 pages.

Codices were read from top to bottom or left to right, but some ran zigzag or clockwise around the page. A priest could "read" the contents quickly, for both the symbols and the colors had meaning. In one situation black meant danger or evil; in another, the direction north. Gods could be identified by their color pattern.

The Mayas also made many codices, but Bishop Landa burned all those stored in the library at Mani, Yucatan. Only three Mayan pre-Conquest codices still exist. All are of great importance and all are in European archives.

OTHER PEOPLES besides the Mayas made codices. Those of the Zapotec-Mixtec were painted on tanned deerskins also coated with lime. These artistic records include a genealogy of Mixtec rulers, but there are some that are still not fully understood.

The Aztecs, too, made thousands of paper codices. One pre-Conquest Aztec codex (p. 92), now in the Museum of Anthropology, tells of Aztec history and of their wanderings before they came to the Valley of Mexico. Most codices were burned by the Spanish. The Indians could never understand why the friars threw codices into the flames and did the same to any Indian found hiding them; a tremendous loss to history.

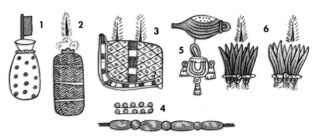

TRIBUTE RECORDED IN AN AZTEC CODEX.

1. 20 bags of cochineal dye
2. 400 bales of cotton
3. 800 blankets
4. 10 jade necklaces
5. 8000 bundles of copal gum
6. 800 bales of feathers

FOR MORE ABOUT THE EARLY PEOPLE OF MEXICO, READ:

Bernal, Ignacio, MEXICO BEFORE CORTEZ: Art, History, Legend. Dolphin Books, New York, 1963. Excellent summary by a Mexican authority.

Caso, Alfonso, THE AZTECS, People of the Sun. U. of Oklahoma Press, Norman, 1958. With Miguel Covarrubias' superb color illustrations.

Morley, Sylvanus G., THE ANCIENT MAYA. Stanford U. Press, Berkeley, 1956. After 20 years, still the standard work on these people.

Peterson, Frederick, ANCIENT MEXICO. Allen and Unwin, London, 1961. A thorough, topical analysis of pre-Hispanic eras.

Wolf, Eric, SONS OF THE SHAKING EARTH. U. of Chicago Press, Chicago, 1959. A summary and evaluation of 3,000 years of Mexican Indian life.

Vaillant, George C., AZTECS OF MEXICO. Penguin, New York, revised 1966. Still the standard work on the Aztecs.

Montezuma sends messengers to Cortes

HISTORICAL MEXICO

The historical period begins with early writing on stelae and later in codices. Practically, it began with Columbus's four voyages. Havana was founded in 1515, and exploration of the Mexican coast soon followed. In 1519, Cortes landed at Veracruz with 555 men and 16 horses. He sank his ten leaky galleons, to prevent desertions.

Enticed by gifts from Montezuma, Cortes moved inland, fighting his way through Tlaxcala, but later making these people his allies. Without the aid of neighboring kingdoms, which had been paying tribute to the Aztecs, Cortes would never have succeeded. He was also able to win over Spanish troops sent to arrest him. Even so, most of his army was killed in the retreat from Tenochtitlan and if the Aztecs had pursued, he would have been destroyed.

Cortes was able to hold Tlaxcala and there received reinforcements of men and weapons. With new allies, he was able to assemble a fleet and attacked Tenochtitlan by land and water. After an 80-day siege, the capital fell, in 1521. Cortes rebuilt the city and sent parties out in all directions to explore and claim the country. In 1528 Cortes returned to Spain to defend himself and his record, leaving an *audencia*, a Spanish court, to govern the country.

Colonial Church at Acatepec

The Church of Tepotzotlan, 1585

THE COLONIAL PERIOD in Mexico lasted nearly 300 years and slowly produced great changes in the country. Two *audiencias* (courts) gave way to government by viceroys (deputies of the king). A total of 61 of them governed Mexico until independence. The first viceroy, Mendoza, instigated a policy of exploration which sent men like de Leon, de Soto, de Vaca, and Coronado far into what is now the U.S. Mendoza (and the second *audiencia* before him) tried to set up laws for the protection of the Indians. For a while the Indians' communal lands were inviolate. But, as the Crown gave out more and more large estates (*encomiendas*), this communal land was absorbed. Much later land gradually passed to the Church, which ended up as owner of more than half the land and wealth of Mexico.

THE CHURCH was powerful in Mexico in Colonial times, since Church and State were one. The Crown appointed all officers in the regular Church. However, the missionary orders remained under Rome and no priest of the regular Church could interfere with them. During the Colonial period, the Spanish built some 12,000 churches.

The true conquest of Mexico was made by friars of the missionary orders, who went unarmed and unprotected to thousands of villages, to preach, baptize, set up schools and hospitals. One friar, Sahagun, made a detailed study of all aspects of native life. De Gante used native dancing and singing in his services. Indians flocked to the church after an Indian, Juan Diego (in 1531), reported his visions of the Virgin of Guadalupe.

Colonial hacienda

PEOPLE in Colonial Mexico quickly fell into a rigid caste system. At the bottom were the Indians who worked their communal lands. They were also peons of the haciendas (above), as were some of the mestizos (those of mixed Indian and Spanish ancestry). Mestizos also worked the mines; some were craftsmen. Higher up the ladder were the Creoles—men of Spanish ancestry, but born in Mexico.

Creoles held secondary positions in government and the Church; some were landlords; many lived on income from haciendas. At the top were Spaniards, born in Spain. This ruling class, through government or Church, controlled the wealth and the land. Spaniards were also merchants and contractors. This social stratification was quick in building, but gave way very slowly.

WORK in the fields, mines, and factories was a heavy burden on the mestizos and Indians, who were often no better than slaves. European diseases—tuberculosis, smallpox, and measles (to which the Indians had no immunity)—killed thousands. The pre-Conquest population of Mexico was estimated at five to nine million. By 1600 it was less than three million.

The mining of silver and gold became the only industry getting government support, since one-fifth of these metals went to the Crown. The mines more than doubled the world's supply of silver. Much of that shipped to Spain was seized by English and Dutch pirates: Drake, Hawkins, Raleigh, and others. Colonial life seemed smooth, but internal strains, inequalities, and class hatred smoldered.

British ships attack Spanish galleons

COLONIAL MONUMENTS abound in Mexico. Most are religious—churches, cathedrals, convents. The rest are public buildings, and a few haciendas. A nominal entrance fee is charged. Entire towns have been preserved as national monuments. These are well maintained under government control and a number are restored. Visit some of those listed alphabetically below. Check road maps for distance and directions. The National Institute of Anthropology and History has illustrated guides to important monuments, in Spanish and in English.

ACOLMAN: a 16th-century Augustine convent considered the best example of fortress-convent architecture. Near Teotihuacan.

ACTOPAN: has another 16th-century convent in an Indian town.

CAMPECHE: has old walls and bastions; a 17th-century cathedral; a regional museum and an old colonial bridge with stone dogs.

CELAYA: San Francisco Church (1629) with altars designed later by Tresguerras, the noted architect-painter, buried here.

CHAPINGO: an old hacienda, now National School of Agriculture. The old church is now the auditorium.

CHOLULA: in an area of many churches. Visit two: the rebuilt church of Los Remedios, atop the great pyramid, and the 16th-century Church of San Gabriel with its chapel of 49 domes.

CUERNAVACA: 16th-century Cathedral and Palace of Cortes (now state capitol). Borda Gardens (18th century) are worth a look.

GUADALAJARA: state capitol, museum, and a Cathedral are 17th-century buildings. Extensive suburbs with colonial homes.

GUANAJUATO: (founded 1534) a rich colonial mining center. See La Parroquia and the ornate La Valenciana Church.

HUEJOTZINGO: fortress-convent, 16th century. Has fine stone sculpture, retablos, and black-and-white murals.

MERIDA: (founded 1542), 16th-century Cathedral and Casa de Montejo (1549), home of the conqueror of Yucatan.

MORELIA: (founded 1541) Colegio San Nicholas, second college in New World. Church of San Francisco (1531). See also the 17th-century Cathedral and the old aqueduct (1785).

OAXACA: Cathedral (16th–18th century); Santo Domingo, a 16th-century fortress-convent, very ornate, and Basilica de la Soledad, another 16th-century shrine of black stone.

OZUMBA: near Popo, a 16th-century Franciscan convent with murals showing first missionaries being received by Cortes.

PATZCUARO: a restored colonial town with hilly, cobblestone streets. See San Francisco Church and La Colegiata; also Casa del Gigante— an interesting old house in the plaza.

PUEBLA: (founded 1531) is a city of old tiled buildings. See the Cathedral (16th–17th century) with many chapels and fine carvings; Biblioteca Palafoxiana, a very old library, located near the Cathedral; Casa de Alfenique, a colonial home, now a regional museum.

QUERETARO: (1531) Church of San Francisco and adjoining Museum Pio Mariana with 18th-century books; also churches of Santa Clara and Santa Rosa (17th century).

SAN CRISTOBAL DE LAS CASAS: (founded 1528), a colonial and Indian city. See market, Cathedral, and Santo Domingo Church.

SAN LUIS POTOSI: a modern city with a 17th-century Cathedral. State capitol (1770). Teatro Alarcon and Caja de Agua are two of many buildings designed and decorated by Francisco Tresguerras (born 1765), noted architect-painter.

SAN MIGUEL ALLENDE: (founded 1542) is a colonial gem and a national monument. Visit the plaza and Church of San Francisco.

TAXCO: also a national monument, is an 18th-century silver center with cobblestone streets. See the Church of Santa Prisca; also Casa Figueroa and Casa de Villanueva—colonial houses.

TEPEACA: has one of the first Franciscan convents (1530) and a Moorish tower in the plaza.

TEPOTZOTLAN: a Jesuit convent (1584) and 18th-century church.

TEPOZTLAN: a Dominican 16th-century convent in an Indian town.

TLAXCALA: see San Francisco, oldest church in North America (1521), where Tlaxcalan chiefs were baptized.

TULA: 16th-century fortress-convent with buttressed walls.

YECAPIXTLA: an Augustine convent (1540) near Cuautla.

YURIRIA: the Augustine convent with strong Indian overtones is worth seeing—a national monument, near Morelia.

ZACATECAS: a mining center with a 17th–18th-century Cathedral and other churches. South of town is Convento de Guadalupe (1707), with library and richly decorated chapel.

FEDERAL DISTRICT

In downtown Mexico see the famous Cathedral, begun in the 16th century. Nearby is the National Palace, Monte de Piedad, National Library, Old School of Medicine, Royal Mint, and scores of other over-300-year-old buildings. The House of Tiles, near the Alameda, is now Sanborn's.

Parts of suburban San Ange and Coyoacan have retained narrow, cobbled streets and colonial architecture. See the Convent of Carmen (17th century) at San Angel and the Cortes Palace and Dominican Church (16th century) in Coyoacan. Any walk on the old streets is worth taking.

INDEPENDENCE was in the air sparked by the American and French revolutions and fueled by hatreds and jealousies in the class system; the tight colonial economy; the prevalent alienation and the bone-deep poverty of Indians and mestizos.

MIGUEL HIDALGO was a Creole parish priest at Dolores, Guanajuato. He had a taste for gambling and the secret "literary" societies to which most intellectuals belonged. His concern for the Indians led him to develop several new local industries.

With Ignacio Allende, local military commander, a revolution and proclamation of independence was planned for Dec. 8, 1810. News leaked out, however, and the crisis forced Hidalgo to a quick decision. He rang the church bells, rallied the people on Sept. 16, and called for their support against the Spanish. Hidalgo's motley army took San Miguel, Celaya, and Morelia. They were defeated by government troops in Jan. 1811. Hidalgo and Allende retreated north but were captured and shot in July. Their defeat did not end the revolution.

JOSE MARIA MORELOS, a priest and pupil of Hidalgo, continued to fight after Hidalgo and Allende were executed. A better tactician and leader, he harassed the Spanish troops for a year. When bottled up in Cuautla, he managed to escape. In Nov. 1812, his troops took Oaxaca. The next year Morelos prepared a congress that came up with a statement of independence and human rights. Later, his army took up positions in the hills around Morelia, where the government troops under Agustin de Iturbide rushed out and defeated them. Morelos fought delaying actions before he was captured and executed.

Other revolutionists kept on fighting. Lopez Rayon and Nicolas Bravo were captured in 1817. Vincent Guerrero held on through 1818–19, when the tide finally turned against Spain.

DOÑA LEONA VICARIO wife of the mayor of Queretaro, conspired with her husband to aid Hidalgo and Allende plot the revolution. Learning that the scheme had been discovered, she warned Hidalgo who changed his plans on the spot and called for the revolution on Sept. 16, instead of in December as had been planned. From a mural by Juan O'Gorman.

AGUSTIN DE ITURBIDE rose to power after a complete political turnover. As a by-product of the Napoleonic wars, a liberal constitution for Mexico was written in 1812, but it did not become effective till 1820. Conservatives in Mexico now talked independence, fearful of a liberal regime, new taxes, and loss of privileges. This conservative group asked the viceroy to send Iturbide south, in 1820, to clean up the remnants of the liberal rebels.

Iturbide's forces were defeated by Guerrero, who invited Iturbide to join him. The two armies finally merged and Iturbide issued his Plan of Iguala, which called for independence and a constitutional monarchy. Generals and liberals rallied to the plan. The insurgent armies entered Mexico City on Sept. 27, 1821, and proclaimed independence. Iturbide pressured congress to make him emperor. Then he dissolved congress. But with opposing republican armies on the way, he abdicated and was executed. In 1824, a federal constitution was adopted and a president elected.

Iturbide's coronation robe was patterned on that of Napoleon.

A LOST CENTURY might label the period 1820–1920, for independence left Mexico with many problems that took a century to solve. Foreign intervention continued. The internal struggle between liberals and conservatives remained, as did internal economic, educational, health, and conservation problems.

IN THE FIFTY YEARS that followed Iturbide, Mexico changed rulers at a prodigious pace—two emperors, 40 presidents, and at least a dozen provisional or caretaker governments. In addition, she lost half her territory to the U.S. (see map below). The province of Texas, with aid from U.S. settlers, won independence in 1836. In 1845, after Texas became a state, war broke out again.

The war was marked by unusual incidents, such as the Irish company that deserted the U.S. Army to join the Mexicans (most were later captured and executed). In a last stand, a corps of cadets defended Chapultepec Castle. They are now *los niños heroes.*

Antonio Lopez de Santa Anna doffed his general's sword 11 times to become President. With losses in the field and on the political front about equal, Santa Anna has been blamed for this disastrous period. The Treaty of Guadalupe ceded Mexico's northern lands to the U.S. for 15 million pesos. After the war, Santa Anna was in and out of office, until exiled in 1855.

Mexico's Lost Territory, 1836–1853

Treaty of Guadalupe— Hidalgo, 1848

Gadsden Purchase, 1853

Texas, 1836

Republic of Mexico

BENITO JUAREZ, an orphaned Zapotec boy from Oaxaca, learned to read from a friar. He went on to a law degree and became governor, only to be exiled by Santa Anna. Returning in 1855, he led his people against the French and the conservatives.

A NEW PLAN—the Plan of Ayutla—rallied the liberals against Santa Anna. Ignacio Commonfort, author of the plan, became President. New laws restricted church property and, in 1857, a new constitution was adopted that clearly granted freedom of religion in Mexico. Benito Juarez became Commonfort's Vice President.

Conservative revolt against the new constitution was quick. Commonfort fled and conservative generals took over. But Juarez, in Veracruz, continued to gain support. The conservatives were routed, and in 1861, Juarez entered Mexico City. But without funds he had little control over the army and its looting.

Juarez "froze" Mexico's overwhelming foreign debts. This act gave Napoleon III an opportunity to push French claims, while the U.S. was deadlocked in its Civil War. A trained French Army came but was roundly defeated at Puebla, May 5, 1862. Next year French reinforcements, under a new general, captured Puebla and the capital. Juarez fled, but carried on from his old black coach. Napoleon III sent the naive Maximilian and Carlotta to Mexico, where they ruled for three years. When most of the French Army left in 1867, Juarez moved against Maximilian and his remaining troops. At Queretaro, Maximilian was executed.

Juarez and his coach.

Juarez monument in the Alameda, Mexico City.

A UNITED MEXICO was the fruit of the Juarez government. Each step forward was planned to this end. Schools were started; finances reorganized. But in his methodical progress, Juarez made enemies of the generals. The election of 1871 was a three-way tie. Congress declared Juarez the winner. Porfirio Diaz, one of the losers, revolted, but his revolt in Oaxaca was quickly put down. In July 1872, Juarez died at his desk of a heart attack.

MEXICO MOURNED Juarez, who has often been compared to Abraham Lincoln, as a person and leader. Lerdo, the Vice President, took office and offered amnesty to political prisoners. He gave Diaz a new start and tried hard to be popular. But he was no Juarez. When Lerdo ran for reelection in 1876, Diaz set forth his Plan of Tuxtepec for "effective suffrage and no reelection." Discontented generals joined him.

Diaz attacked Monterrey, only to be defeated. Diaz fled to New York. He later returned in disguise, via Veracruz, to join his friends in Oaxaca. Diaz raised an army and, taking advantage of troubles in the capital, fought his way into Mexico City. Lerdo stuffed his pockets and fled. Diaz was elected President in 1877

PORFIRIO DIAZ brought his friends into the government and won over enemies with jobs for all. He welcomed foreign capital and control by large corporations. Diaz organized a national police force for rual areas—the *rurales*—which soon became an organization of subsidized bandits.

In 1880, his term expired and Diaz stepped down, after putting a hand-picked politician, Manuel Gonzalez, in the presidential chair. During his four years in office, Gonzalez came close to despoiling Mexico. He sold millions of acres of land and mineral rights to foreign corporations. By the time his term was over, even Diaz was disgusted. Despite his slogan of "no reelection," Diaz ran again. He was reelected and held office till 1910.

ECONOMIC ADVANCE was the aim of Diaz, and in the 34 years he controlled Mexico there was much that could be labeled progress. The capital was beautified with large parks and broad avenues. The Palace of Fine Arts and many monuments were erected. Diaz encouraged art and science. He governed with the aid of technical advisers who were quickly labeled "scientists."

Under their supervision great programs of public works were instituted. Railroads were enlarged by 9,000 miles; heavy industry, textiles, and agriculture increased their output. Foreign trade jumped ten-fold. Banks redoubled in number and in capital. Mexico's overall prosperity raised its position among nations and established its credit abroad. This side of the picture was rosy, indeed. But it was only one part.

ON THE OTHER SIDE was calamity. Mexico's natural resources were squandered at a prodigious rate, with little of the income reaching Mexicans. The Church recovered some of its former lands and privileges. Over 130 million acres of public land were lost, and by 1910 less than a thousand families owned 90% of Mexico, mainly as great haciendas. Nine million Mexicans were landless. The peons on the haciendas earned 120 pesos a year but were always deep in debt to the company store—a debt that was passed on from father to son. The country was split between wealth and poverty.

In the capital, advisers of Diaz were worried. Nearing eighty, he had picked no successor. His Vice President was despised and the storm of revolution was fast approaching.

Palace of Fine Arts, Mexico City

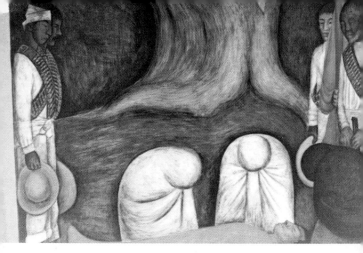

Revolution, a mural by *Diego Rivera, Chapingo*

THE REVOLUTION OF 1910 led to the constitution of 1917, and this became the foundation of modern Mexico. It all began when Porfirio Diaz, who had already served six terms as President, decided to run again after his announced retirement. Francisco Madero set up an anti-reelection party and began a vigorous campaign. Thousands of people were caught up by the idea but not Diaz, who jailed Madero a month before the July election and then counted himself the overwhelming victor, when the returns came in.

MADERO, released from prison in October, fled to San Antonio, where he published his Plan of San Luis Potosi calling for a revolution on November 20, 1910. The response was so meager that Madero was preparing to flee again, when he heard of a successful uprising in Chihuahua, led by Pasqual Orozco and Pancho Villa. Madero promptly joined them, and the rebel army soon captured Ciudad Juarez.

Meanwhile, Emiliano Zapata, demanding land reform, had raised a peon army in Morelos. As the uprisings grew, Diaz resigned in May 1911 and went into exile. Victorious Madero entered the capital, called for honest elections and was elected President in October. But Madero did not make reforms sweeping or rapid enough. Zapata, unhappy because land reform was slow, renewed his revolt. A nephew of Diaz, with conservative backing, began another. The U.S. ambassador conspired to make Victoriano Huerta, Madero's wayward general, Mexico's President.

Madero and his Vice President were arrested and murdered. Huerta was proclaimed President and held office for 17 months, while Zapata, Villa, and two new leaders, Alvaro Obregon and Venustiano Carranza, led forces against him. The upshot was five years of war and U.S. intervention.

Pitched battles killed thousands of Mexicans and destroyed badly needed property. In 1917, a new constitution, written under the guidance of Carranza and Obregon, set up a pattern for social as well as political reform. But war was not over. Obregon defeated Villa, who, in turn, terrorized the northern border.

Again the U.S. sent troops into Mexico and again the result was to unite that country against the Yankees. Carranza held onto the presidency till 1920, when he, too, was murdered. A change of feeling brought Dwight Morrow to Mexico as U.S. ambassador. He improved relationships between the governments and helped to dispel much of the earlier bitterness.

The PRI today is the controlling political party in Mexico. Although a few minor opposition parties exist, most elected officials are members of the PRI.

Brown Bros.

Pancho Villa

Meanwhile Obregon's term as President and that of his successor, Calles, were marked by rebellions, though both exerted dictatorial power. Obregon, reelected after Calles, was soon assassinated. Calles kept control behind the scenes from 1928–36. He created the National Revolutionary Party (PNR), and nominated Lazaro Cardenas for President in 1934.

Cardenas pushed ahead with social and political reform. All elections since have put responsible men in office. The PNR has become the Party of Revolutionary Institutions (PRI).

A SUMMARY OF MEXICAN HISTORY

800	Mayan and several other civilizations at their peak.
1325	Aztecs found Tenochtitlan, their capital.
1519	Cortes lands at Veracruz, to explore and conquer.
1521	Fall of Tenochtitlan, now Zocalo area of Mexico City.
1521– 1640	Missionary orders convert Indians and wield great power.
1548	Discovery of silver begins a century-long period of mining and metal exploitation.
1754	Virgin of Guadalupe declared patroness of Mexico by papal bull.
1803	Humboldt explores and publicizes Mexico.
1810–11	Hildalgo leads first revolt against Spain.
1812–15	Morelos leads another unsuccessful revolt.
1821	Independence achieved by Iturbide, who is proclaimed emperor. This begins a century of unrest.
1824	First constitution sets up a federal government.
1832–55	Santa Anna president 11 times.
1836	Texas wins independence from Mexico.
1845–48	War with U.S. leads to loss of half of Mexican territory.
1857	New constitution separates church from state.
1858–72	Benito Juarez president; war of reform.
1864–67	French intervention; Maximilian rules and dies.
1867	Railroad from Veracruz to Mexico City completed.
1876– 1910	Porfirio Diaz president and dictator; rapid economic growth, loss of communal Indian lands, creating landless peons; rise of haciendas.
1910–11	Revolt by Madero aided by Villa and Zapata.
1913	Huerta becomes president after U.S. intervention; Villa, Obregon, and Zapata continue revolution.
1914–16	U.S. withdraws; Obregon enters Mexico City; internal warfare with Villa and Calles.
1917	New constitution stresses right to land and resources; introduces program of social welfare.
1921	Obregon as president plans new social program.
1928–34	National Revolutionary Party (PNR) organized and its candidate, Cardenas, is elected. One party system still continues. PNR becomes PRI (Party of Revolutionary Institutions).
1938	Expropriation of oil under 1917 constitution.
1953	Woman suffrage becomes universal in Mexico.
1958	Eleven-year federal education program begins, as does a period of steady economic progress.
1968	Olympic games celebrated in Mexico City.

PEOPLE OF MEXICO TODAY

Mexico's estimated population in 1519 was 5–9 million. Immediately after the Conquest, it was less than 2 million and some 300 years were needed to get back to the 5-million level. Since then, except during the 1910 revolutions, population has boomed. In 20 recent years, the birth rate has been about 45 per thousand; and the population has passed 45 million. Now nearly 60% of the people live in 1,100 cities of over 2,500; over 40% live in over 90,000 villages and rural areas. All this creates new problems for Mexico.

MEXICAN POPULATION

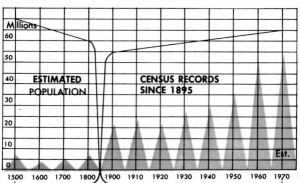

THE POPULATION DENSITY of Mexico and the U.S. is about the same: 20 people per square kilometer. Population distribution patterns are also similar: growing concentrations of people in large cities, shrinking rural populations.

The Federal District of Mexico has about 4,200 persons per sq. km.; so does the District of Columbia. The temperate regions in Mexico average some 20 persons per sq. km., as does a state like Iowa. The arid and tropical regions have about 5 persons per sq. km., the same as Nevada.

The majority of Mexico's population is now urban. It is increasing at the rate of 1 million (about 3%) annually. This explosion worries Mexicans, as it does governments the world over. Programs for soil improvement, irrigation, and industrialization help. As yet, efforts toward better health, education, and living conditions, mandatory for progress, cannot keep up with the growing needs. Demographic experts and government officials are working hard on these problems.

MEXICO, as a nation, is a happy union of many peoples of many different cultures and languages. Its population can be blocked roughly into whites, mestizos, and Indians, with a few Asians and Africans. In modern Mexico, economic status, personal ability, and education are the social determinants rather than racial origin.

WHITES (*blancos*), who make up some 15% of the population, are mainly of Spanish origin, though many generations removed. Only a few are descendants of immigrants from other parts of Europe and the Middle East.

Next to those of Spanish origin are North Americans, who make up the largest group of foreigners in Mexico today. Some have become Mexican citizens. *Residentes,* who maintain their U.S. citizenship, are welcomed and come in increasing numbers. Most, who fall into this group, live in or near cities. They are the well-to-do. In this group are industrialists, professionals, and retired people.

MINORITY GROUPS have found refuge in Mexico for well over a century. Indians from the U.S. (Pima, Papago, Apache, and Kickapoo), pressured by our white settlers, crossed the border and now live in northern Mexico.

The large number of Irish, who arrived after the potato famine of 1846, have long been integrated into the population, although Irish names still persist.

More recently, Russians, Poles, Spanish, Germans, Austrians, Cubans, and Guatemaltecans have come to live in Mexico. A small number of Asians (about 1%), now settled in Mexico, are mostly tradesmen in small, often rural communities.

A mestizo family picnicking in the country with their Indian hosts.

MESTIZOS, the backbone of Mexico's population (76%), are descendants of Indians and Spaniards. Although many bear old Spanish names, such as Gonzales, Jimenez, Montoya, all are Mexicans and proud of it.

These Mexicans live everywhere. They are farmers, factory workers, and merchants, filling both skilled and unskilled positions and nearly all government posts. They are the core of the professions: doctors, lawyers, writers, teachers, artists, architects, and engineers.

From the mestizos has emerged Mexico's new middle class. To the personal efforts and abilities of this group, Mexico owes much of its present rapid progress.

INDIANS today make up about 8% of the population. Most live in the southern half of Mexico; the remainder in the extreme north.

The name *Indios,* however, is not often used. Tribal and group names, such as Tlaxcalan, Otomi, Mixtec, and Maya, are preferred. Today, most native groups live in self-governing villages and work as farmers, herders, miners, and artisans. Men may still wear homemade white cottons and *huaraches* (sandals).

These rural Mexicans fill unskilled jobs and work as domestics in cities. But they gradually adopt city ways and dress, and take advantage of the better schooling their children can get.

Siouan

Athabascan

Nahuatl

Otomi, Mixtec, Zapotec

Mayan

SPANISH is the language of Mexico, yet Indian languages number well over a hundred. Most can be fitted into five language groups, shown on the above map. Each tribal language has an extensive vocabulary of several thousand words, and a rich oral tradition of myths and legends, often associated with ancient religions.

Today, for example, some six Indian languages are spoken in Puebla; nine, in Oaxaca; seven, in Chiapas. Nahuatl, a language of the Nahua group, was the speech of the Aztec conquerors and, after 1200, spread throughout their domain (p. 93). Many conquered tribes took on Nahuatl,

gradually losing their own tongue. Nahuatl was the first Mexican language adapted to Latin script by the Spanish. It is now spoken by some 700,000 Indians. Mayan is spoken by close to a half million people, as is Otomi.

Most Indians also speak Spanish, though many Indian youngsters still learn Spanish as a second language. With compulsory education, children quickly learn to read and write. Older Indians often lack these skills. Well over half of them are still nonliterate. But through adult education classes and with the help of young bilingual teachers, illiteracy among Indians as well as mestizos is being reduced.

REGIONALISM is still a strong social factor, making for great variations in Mexican life. Mexico's distinctive regions are due in part to its terrain, which tends to isolate groups and make them self-sufficient, and in part to its heritage from independent Indian states. Regional differences are manifest in languages and customs, in homes, furnishings, foods, dress, and the arts and crafts. If you cannot visit villages, see the excellent ethnographic exhibits at the National Museum of Anthropology.

HOMES in rural areas are often the traditional one-room, single-family shelter. Building materials vary with the climate, locale, and a family's means. Houses of adobe (sun-dried bricks of clay and straw) are most common, especially in the cool highlands. Below (1) is one under construction. Tropical lowland homes are built of poles with woven, matted walls and thatched roofs (2).

Where ample wood is available, as in Michoacan, houses are of boards with shingled roofs (3).

The traditional village or town home of the more well-to-do shows Spanish influence. It is of adobe or stone, built around an enclosed patio, with space for an extended family. The heavy street door and barred windows assure total privacy for household activities within (4).

Mole

Enchiladas

Tortilla

Chiles Rellenos

Tamales

FOOD Corn, beans, and chili are the staples of the rural Mexican diet. With fish, meat, fowl, rice, fresh fruits, vegetables, cactus pods, and wild plants, these staples are combined into a variety of nutritious and spicy (*picante*) dishes. Many are traditional, with typical regional variations. *Tortillas* are the universal thin "pancakes" of ground corn, eaten steaming hot with every meal. *Tacos* are fried tortillas, filled with meat, tomato, chili and onions. *Enchiladas* are baked tortillas, filled with meat and steeped in sauce. *Tamales* are a baked corn meal with meat and chili, folded in corn husks or banana leaves. *Frijoles* are dark beans, cooked and ground to a paste, with onions and cheese. Chili peppers are eaten as a vegetable or a sauce. *Mole*, an Indian sauce, is made of chocolate, chili, and herbs. Drinks include herb tea (*manzanilla*), chocolate, coffee, and *pulque*.

REGIONAL DRESS, varied and often sumptuous, is still worn at rural fiestas and at parties and dances by the urban middle class. Today the most colorful regional dress is found in Oaxaca (p. 117), Chiapas and Yucatan (p. 119), and among the Huichol and Seri (p. 119).

Stately Tehuantepec women wear elaborate and expensive garments of cotton and silk, with a pleated white head shawl (*mantilla*) of lace. The long dress is embroidered in bold flower designs.

By comparison, the long smock (*huipil*) from Yalalog is modest. Bright tassels of rayon thread are a typical decoration. The wraparound skirt is of heavy, handwoven cotton. A Chinantec *huipil* more elaborate, is embroidered in geometric, flower, and animal designs.

Oaxacan men's everyday dress is of the traditional heavy, white *manta*: loose-fitting trousers, tied at the waist, and a buttoned-down, long-sleeved shirt. Over this homemade garment the thick, wool *serape* is essential, for Oaxacan highlands are cold (p. 129).

The Taquate costume is similar to the Chiapas Indian's. The homespun cotton shorts are embroidered. Over this is a long, decorated shirt, tucked in at the waist, to serve as a much-needed pocket or pouch.

Taquate

Oaxaca

Chinantec

Yalalog

Tehuantepec

117

Charro

China
Poblana

hat dance

THE CHARRO dancer (above) is named for his Mexican "cowboy" costume. *Charro* means flashy in Spanish. The suit, an adaptation of the Spanish bolero jacket and tight trousers is worn by clubs of amateur weekend horsemen.

The lady's dress, called *China poblana,* meaning Chinese of Puebla, is a folk costume, too. The costume was supposedly designed by a Chinese slave girl in Puebla.

The men come from villages near San Cristobal. Shorts and blouse (plain or decorated) are worn under a wool serape. Hats are decorated with gay ribbons, intended to denote a man's status—married or single.

In Yucatan, a woman's dress retains a pre-Spanish style with modifications. Always snow white, it is machine- or elaborately hand-embroidered and is worn with a lace-edged petticoat.

The Seri women of northwestern Mexico dress in a long, wide skirt and cotton blouse, similar to the dress of our Apache Indians. They still tattoo their faces and use feathers and bird skins for decoration.

The Huichol highlanders' garment is of homespun cotton, worked with elaborate bands of colored embroidery. Each man wears a string of small pouches and bags—all finely hand-loomed and decorated.

118

Chiapas

Chiapas

Yucatan

Seri

Huichol

FIESTAS in Mexico are many. They include national, local, and religious festivities, with processions (often solemn), regional costumes, dancing, music (marimbas), always fireworks, and sometimes bullfights. The gaiety is enhanced with flowers, confetti, refreshments, and (in season) *piñata* parties in homes. Every town and village has several fiestas during the year. Usually one of these honors the patron saint. Watch for local announcements. Fiestas usually start at the town plaza. A market and sometimes a fair may be held at the same time.

Larger towns have displays, pageants, and floats, several bands and folk dancers. Rural communities have more modest fiestas. Days of devoted labor produce home-made decorations and just as much fun and noise.

Dates for fiestas may vary. It is advisable to check dates, distances, roads, available transportation, and accommodations. At a fiesta, the discreet visitor should also make sure whether, as an outsider, he is to get into things or to remain a quiet observer.

THE MOST IMPORTANT NATIONAL AND
POPULAR HOLIDAYS,

Celebrated widely on dates indicated, are:

Jan. 1: New Year's Day. Carnivals throughout the land.

Jan. 6: Day of the Wisemen. Gifts exchanged, as on Christmas, especially gifts for children.

Feb. 2: *La Candelaria* (Candlemas). Animals and seeds are blessed.

Mar. 21: Birthday of Benito Juarez—Indian Child's Day (special fiesta in Oaxaca, birthplace of Juarez).

Mar. or Apr.: Three days prior to Ash Wednesday are days of Mardi Gras, combined with spring and the pre-Lent holidays. The last week of Lent is *Semana Santa* (Holy Week), which begins with Palm Sunday. On Good Friday some villages still enact the Crucifixion—a solemn occasion. Easter Sunday with festivities and fireworks brings the Lenten season to an end. Check dates and locations.

May 1: National Labor Day. Parades and civic ceremonies.

May 3: Day of the Holy Cross (*Santa Cruz*). A special holiday for builders. Huge crosses, decorated with flowers and papier-mâché, displayed over new buildings.

Local Fiesta, in the school grounds, Tlaxcala.

May 5: *Cinco de Mayo.* Defeat of the French in 1867. Special fiesta in Puebla.

Late May or early June: Corpus Christi. Processions, flowers, music.

Aug. 15: Day of Assumption. Fairs and bullfights.

Sept. 15–16: Independence Day. Political speeches, parades, and floats. Everyone gathers at the plaza (Zocalo in Mexico City). The mayor, governor, or president speaks. Fireworks.

Oct. 12: Day of the Races *(Dia de la Raza).* Schoolchildren parade with flags of all nations. In Mexico City wreaths are laid at Columbus' monument.

Nov. 1–2: All Saints' Day and All Souls' Day—mourning days with masses in all churches, flowers (especially marigolds), and religious plays. Women and children visit cemeteries with food offerings, sugar skulls and angels. All-night vigil with lighted candles and fires.

Nov. 20: Commemorates the Revolution of 1910. Parades. Wreaths placed at monuments of the nation's heroes.

Dec. 12: Guadalupe Day, with special events at the Virgin of Guadalupe Shrine (Villa Madero, Mexico City). Pilgrims, regional costumes, dances, music.

Dec. 16–24: Christmas festivities, with songs and lighted candles. Neighborly processions to homes *(posadas).* Break the paper-decorated clay pots *(piñatas)* filled with candies and fruits.

Dec. 25: Christmas. Instead of a Christmas tree, Mexicans set up a small manger with clay figurines of the Holy Family and animals.

LOCAL AND RELIGIOUS FIESTAS. The most numerous are on:

June 13: San Antonio's Day	**Aug. 25:** San Bartholome
June 24: San Juan	**Sept. 29:** San Michel
June 29: San Pedro and San Paul	**Oct. 4:** San Francisco
July 20–27: Special events in Oaxaca	**Nov. 25:** Santa Catarina
July 25: Señor Santiago	**Nov. 30:** San Andres

Ceramic plaques and pots at Metepec, a craft village.

POPULAR ARTS AND HANDICRAFTS

Popular arts and handicrafts are an inherent part of Mexican life. Basketry, pottery, weaving, and wood, stone, leather, and feather work long antedate the Conquest, as do such art forms as murals, frescoes, and sculpture. With better Spanish looms, weaving increased; so did work with gold, silver, copper, and iron. Pottery was glazed and glass was made. Now time is taking its toll and centuries of handwork may be slowly coming to an end. Visitors can contribute in encouraging authentic popular arts and handicrafts of good materials and design.

FOR MORE ABOUT MEXICO'S POPULAR ARTS, READ:

Grove, Richard, MEXICAN POPULAR ARTS TODAY. Taylor Museum, Colorado Springs, 1954.

Ross, Patricia F., MADE IN MEXICO. Knopf, New York, 1952. An excellent overview of Mexico's crafts, with historical backgrounds.

Toor, Frances, A TREASURY OF MEXICAN FOLKWAYS. Crown, New York, 1947. Comprehensive, popular treatment for tourists.

t'Serstevens, A., MEXICO, THREE-STOREYED LAND. Bobbs-Merrill, Indianapolis. A Frenchman's impressions.

Yucatan

Chiapas

Oaxaca

BASKETMAKING,

which may have antedated both pottery and weaving, is still universal. Rush, cane, bamboo, maguey, and willow are woven into containers of all sizes, shapes, and colors, and into mats *(petates)*, wicker furniture, toys, and pocketbooks. A rural household has many simple storage and marketing baskets, plus the indispensable *petates*. Markets and stores have baskets, table mats, and ornaments for tourists. Some are tightly woven in natural colors. Beware of shoddy work and gaudy colors that fade.

Toluca

Queretaro

Seri

Guerrero

Tarahumara

MODERN POTTERY reflects traditional regional designs developed in scores of pottery-making villages. These beautiful patterns are easy to recognize. After the Spanish introduced the potter's wheel, glazing, and improved kilns, pottery was further refined and developed with a new flair for color, design, and decoration. From Spain also came the idea for hand-painted glazed tiles, still made in Puebla. The thick, red, roof tiles are local.

Ceramic pots, inexpensive and decorative, are essentials in rural households. Rural Mexicans believe food prepared in clay pots has an added flavor. Although metal and plastic housewares are available in every market, the housewife and tourist find it hard to resist the colorful conglomeration, pile upon pile and row upon row, of jugs, pots, vases, pitchers (ollas), bowls, plates, cups, and frying pans (comales).

OAXACAN (above) jet-black pottery is well designed and easily recognized. Tourist pieces may be poorly fired, intended more for decoration than utility.

METEPEC, and Matamoros de Izucar, craftsmen make colorful, elaborate candlesticks with figures, animals, and other elements. The bright colors fade.

TONALA AND TLAQUEPAQUE (both near Guadalajara) make colorful birds and animals. Tlaquepaque also makes many kinds of decorated and glazed pottery.

PUEBLA'S famous multicolored pottery and tiles are still popular today. Puebla also makes a less elaborate ware—with colonial designs—and less expensive.

GUANAJUATO makes cream and dark-brown tableware, with a green glaze on the inside. Rather heavy, but durable and sometimes of good, simple design.

PATZCUARO (and vicinity). Cream-colored ware with simple painted designs in brown and green. Dishes, platters, and 3-legged pots, often unglazed.

124

Puebla tiles

Guanajuato

Puebla

Tonala & Tlaquepaque

Puebla

Metepec

Guanajuato

Metepec

Patzcuaro and vicinity

Patzcuaro

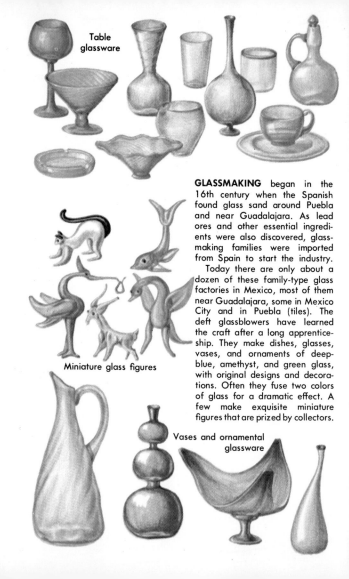

Table glassware

Miniature glass figures

GLASSMAKING began in the 16th century when the Spanish found glass sand around Puebla and near Guadalajara. As lead ores and other essential ingredients were also discovered, glassmaking families were imported from Spain to start the industry.

Today there are only about a dozen of these family-type glass factories in Mexico, most of them near Guadalajara, some in Mexico City and in Puebla (tiles). The deft glassblowers have learned the craft after a long apprenticeship. They make dishes, glasses, vases, and ornaments of deep-blue, amethyst, and green glass, with original designs and decorations. Often they fuse two colors of glass for a dramatic effect. A few make exquisite miniature figures that are prized by collectors.

Vases and ornamental glassware

Pouch—Oaxaca

Saddle—Central Mexico

Machete and Sheath Guerrero

LEATHERWORK in Mexico came with Spanish cattle and horses. It developed into a craft for making saddles, bridles, and pouches (often with elaborate tooling and silver trimmings), as well as sturdy *huaraches*, belts, bags, holsters, and thongs. Leatherwork is still important in smaller towns. Look for locally made boots, shoes, wallets, and tooled novelties.

headdress—Oaxaca

Purse and belt—Mexico City

FEATHERWORK is now a lost art. The bright feathers of tropical birds were valued by Indians who made magnificent feather capes and headdresses. Feather-inlay "paintings" were common. Mexican conservation laws now protects wild birds. Only a few novelties and greeting cards now use dyed feathers of domestic birds.

Feather cards—Mexico

Huaraches—Jalisco

127

Handloom Weaving—Oaxaca

WEAVING in pre-Conquest times was universal in Mexico but was confined to cotton, rushes, maguey, and pounded bark fibers. The Spanish brought sheep and goats and the upright loom. This stimulated weaving of wool cloth, rugs, and *serapes*, the traditional outer garment for men. It is woven, rug-shaped, in one or two pieces, cut to slip over the head.

Current weaving, influenced by tourist demands, produces a variety of cotton fabrics of striking colors looms. Quality varies. Dyes are often poor. Better weaving with fast dyes comes from a cooperative at Uruapan.

MANTA, the local cotton, like unbleached muslin, is often dyed in striking colors. The material below is from Toluca. On p. 129 are typical woven handicrafts. Rugs and *serapes* of good weave and wool are still made locally and in centers, like Tlaxcala.

Decorated shirts come from Patzcuaro, Puebla, and Oaxaca, which also produces heavy wool skirts (*faldas*) of fine double weave. Excellent weaving is found also in and around San Cristobal— local costumes, *serapes* of several designs, and wool cloth.

Hand-loomed cottons, Uruapan

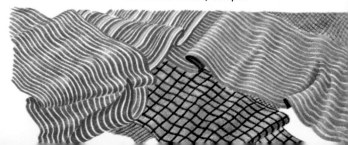

Huichol

Uruapan

Uruapan

Patzcuaro

Patzcuaro

Tlaxcala

Puebla

Patzcuaro

Huejotzingo

Oaxaca

129

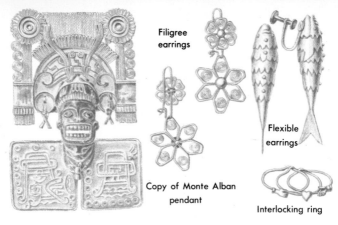

Filigree earrings

Flexible earrings

Copy of Monte Alban pendant

Interlocking ring

Goldwork from Oaxaca

GOLD AND SILVER, skillfully worked for centuries, had intrinsic value only as ornaments to the Indians. When the Spaniards seized Mexico's wealth, the beautifully wrought ornaments and religious objects (pp. 19, 85) were melted down. The workings were seized and expanded by the large-scale use of slave labor. Gold and silver poured into Spain. Much remained in Mexico as bullion and as gold and silver offerings in the churches.

Later came the gold and silver *milagros*. These cast representations of people, arms, legs, heads, houses, animals, etc. are left at the church with a prayer for a miraculous cure.

Stimulated by William Spratling, Taxco (site of old silver mines) became the silver craft center of Mexico about 1940, a position it still holds. Its craftsmen also work in gold, copper, brass, and "tin." Factories also abound in Mexico City.

GOLDWORK (above) has become increasingly popular since colonial times, as each piece is wealth as well as an ornament. Pre-Columbian pieces, like that from Monte Alban, have been copied in gold (rare), but more often in gilded silver. Their simple design is still unequaled by modern goldsmiths. Another

popular design are the mobile fishes made of a series of circular gold (or silver) plates. Filigree work in gold (and gilded pieces, too) is typical of southern Mexico. Often the work takes the form of earrings, pins, and a few rings. The interlocking rings that fit together to make one ring are a local gold novelty.

130

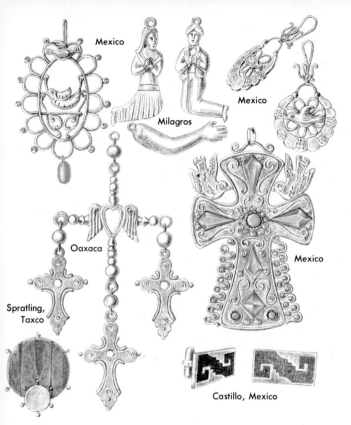

Mexico

Milagros

Mexico

Mexico

Oaxaca

Spratling,
Taxco

Castillo, Mexico

SILVER (p. 19) is now worn much more by tourists than by Mexicans, who prefer gold. Above is a pendant and earrings of classic Mexican design (late 19th century) with three silver *milagros* to be pinned on church draperies. The pendant cross with amethyst and turquoise is another, more elaborate, 19th-century design. The large cross with three pendant crosses is typical of the cast silver made in villages of Oaxaca. It is often seen on a long string of coral (or red glass) beads, interspersed with coins. Most crosses now on sale are copies. Below are modern silver pieces with wood and enamel, made in Mexico City for the tourist trade.

Hand-Hammered Copper

Wrought-iron lamps

COPPER was used in ancient Mexico, but more after the Conquest. Combined with tin, it produced bronze for bells, candlesticks, and cannons. Copperware made in Mexico today comes mainly from Ciudad Escalante, near Patzcuaro. Hand-hammered bowls, pots, pans, trays, and vases are for sale in stores and markets.

IRON, introduced by the Spanish, was quickly adopted for tools, spurs, ornaments, balconies, and furniture. Village blacksmiths made hoes, plows, and other tools. Long steel knives *(machetes)* are used by every farm laborer. Mexican "tinware" (masks, ornaments, and trays) is made from thin "tinned" iron sheets.

"Tin" Mirror

Machete

Tools

132

Masks

Bowl

Gourd

Tray

LACQUER WARE is a native Indian craft made with techniques that resemble those of the Chinese. However, Mexican lacquer is not of Chinese origin. Lacquer is a mixture of turpentine, minerals, and pigments with a resinous sap or with the secretion of scale insects. Craftsmen cover an article with coat after coat of lacquer, each rubbed in by hand. Then they skillfully etch in a design, filling the lines with lac or, by cutting, expose different colored layers beneath.

Lacquer ware centers around Patzcuaro and Uruapan. Olinala, in Guerrero, specializes in bright lacquered chests. More common are lacquered trays, dishes, boxes, carved fruits, and gourds.

Box

Wooden fruits

Tray

Patzcuaro Tray

Olinala Chest

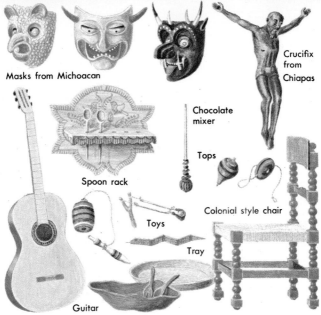

Masks from Michoacan

Crucifix from Chiapas

Chocolate mixer

Tops

Spoon rack

Colonial style chair

Toys

Tray

Guitar

bowl and spoons

WOODWORKING received an added impetus in colonial times. At first Indian, and later, mestizo, craftsmen carved saints and crucifixes. They built and decorated the massive church doors, altars, ceilings, columns, and benches. They also carved the heavy furniture, closets, and chests for Spanish homes. Today some of their best work can be seen in churches, preserved as national monuments, and in the Colonial sections of Mexico's museums.

Village woodcarvers today still make saints and crucifixes. They carve bowls, both simple and decorative, and make wooden spoons and paddles. Carved trays, both simple and lacquered (p. 133), plus boxes, ornaments, and many intriguing toys, are available in markets. Most typical are the *baleros*, a game of skill in which a small tethered barrel is caught on a stick or a tethered ball is caught in a cup.

Some villages are noted for their fine guitars and marimbas. New designers have produced fine furniture for local and tourist markets. Recently, the Colonial style, heavy and solid, has been revived and is enjoying renewed popularity.

Herbs and Vegetables in a Village Market

THE COLORFUL OPEN-AIR MARKETS are fast disappearing, even in rural areas. They are being replaced by sanitary buildings with tiled stalls, running water, and electric lights. Haggling over prices has nearly gone, too. Markets, new and old, sell vegetables, fruits, meats, fish, and prepared foods. Larger markets have sections for dry goods, pottery, baskets, and many small lunch bars.

Markets operate daily, but many towns and villages have one day when the market is larger, richer, and attracts families from miles around. Market day is also a social event, for visiting, gossip, and relaxation.

Open-air restaurant in market

MEXICAN MARKETS provide everyone with food, clothing, and housewares. They afford tourists a chance to
purchase handicrafts. Below are listed selected markets of
interest in Mexico City and within a 100-mile circle.
Special market days are indicated.

MEXICO CITY has scores of local markets. See the following:
   Lagunilla (Plaza Commonfort): large daily market; antiques; Sunday.
   Merced Market (Gen. Anaya): largest and most varied market; daily.
   Sabado Market (San Angel): a tourist wonderland of crafts; Saturday.
   San Juan (Belam & Niño Perdido): large food market with a sepa-
   rate building for crafts and souvenirs; daily.
IXMIQUILPAN: handbags, mats; articles of maguey fiber; Monday.
METEPEC: brightly painted ceramics, animal and flower designs; Monday.
PUEBLA: a general market and a tourist section of handicrafts, ceramics,
   miniatures, special candies; Sunday.
TAXCO: jewelry, silverware, tin and copper articles; serapes, furniture,
   and woodware; Sunday.
TENANCINGO: rebozos, wines, chests of lemonwood; Sunday.
TEXCOCO: wool serapes and rugs; Sunday.
TEXMELUCAN: serapes and woolens from Santa Ana; Tuesday.
TLAXCALA: noted for its wool cloth, rugs, and serapes; Sunday.
TOLUCA: best known to tourists. Products from entire Central Valley
   are assembled here—blankets, rugs, serapes, baskets, mats, pottery,
   embroidered goods; Friday.
XOCHIMILCO: flowers and pottery; Saturday.

OTHER MARKETS OF INTEREST are:
GUADALAJARA: new Liberty Market. Handicrafts from surrounding
   region, hats, baskets, serapes, leather; much pottery and glass.
GUANAJUATO: rebozos, pottery, toys, and baskets.
MERIDA: sisal fiber products: hammocks, purses, mats, bags. Inter-
   esting filigree jewelry.
OAXACA: leather, hand-loomed fabrics, machetes and knives, jewelry,
   pottery from San Bartolo; Saturday.
PAPANTLA: souvenir figurine bottles filled with vanilla, carved turtle
   shells; lace articles made by Totonac Indians.
PATZCUARO: lacquer, jewelry, ceramic animals, woolens, and wood-
   work; Tuesday and Friday.
URUAPAN: lacquered trays, hand-loomed cottons, embroidered table-
   cloths and blouses, woodwork, guitars from nearby Paracho, pottery;
   Sunday.

Monument of the Revolution, from Paseo de la Reforma, Mexico City.

MODERN MEXICO

Modern times, for Mexico, began in 1917 with the present constitution and its guarantees of land and better living. In some 50 years, Mexico has leaped forward, as statistics on industry, agriculture, and health show. The visitor sees better roads, more hotels, and enclosed markets, but may not notice better health and education, improved housing, increased concern for natural resources and international affairs. These are harder to see, but they are equally evident. Finally, modern Mexico still treasures much of the old, historic, and beautiful. Still young, Mexico begins its second fifty years pushing strongly toward its social goals.

FOR MORE ABOUT MODERN MEXICO, READ:

Mateo, Adolfo Lopez (ed.), MEXICO: FIFTY YEARS OF REVOLUTION. Fondo de Cultura Economica, Mexico City, 1963. Clear, expert summaries on progress and problems in many fields. In Spanish.
McHenry, J. P., A SHORT HISTORY OF MEXICO. Doubleday, Garden City, N.Y., 1962. A concise, coherent, chronological history.
Whetten, N., RURAL MEXICO. U. of Chicago Press, Chicago, 1948. A comprehensive, documented, "classic" study.

MEXICO began as a Spanish colony. In the 1600's it was divided into four administrative areas of which Nueva Espana was the largest. Now, Mexico is a democratic federal republic (as established under the Constitution of 1917). It is composed of 29 states, 2 territories, and a Federal District (D.F.). The two territories, Quintana Roo and Baja California (Sur), have the lowest population densities; the Federal District has, by far, the highest. The largest state is Chihuahua, about the size of Wyoming. States are divided into municipalities; territories and the Federal District, into delegations. Mexico's general pattern of government resembles that of the United States.

TOUR MEXICO Air routes connect all the large cities, but you will see more touring by car or by excellent first-class buses. Many and varied organized tours will get you to the tourist "sights." If you drive, try not to average much over a hundred miles a day as you leave to see the real Mexico.

Here are two one-week tours by car. Each day terminates in a city with accommodations, but spend most time along the road. Mileages are in parentheses. Local guide books will give you details.

NORTH. Day 1: from Mexico City to Queretaro (140). Day 2: on to San Miguel Allende (40) to spend afternoon and night. Then, Day 3: via Hidalgo to Guanajuato (55)—a famed old city. Day 4: push on to Guadalajara (175) via Lago de Moreno. Now, south again, Day 5: to Patzcuaro (200) and spend most of Day 6: here. Then, on to Morelia (30) and on Day 7: back to Mexico City (190).

SOUTH. (Try to add an extra day or two) Day 1: via Puebla to Orizaba (185). Day 2: on to Veracruz (50). Now, Day 3: south to Acayucan, the crossroads (155). Then, on Day 4: across the Isthmus to Tehuantepec (135). Next, Day 5: north to Oaxaca (150); see Mitla and Monte Alban. On Day 6: Puebla (240) and on Day 7: back to Mexico City (85).

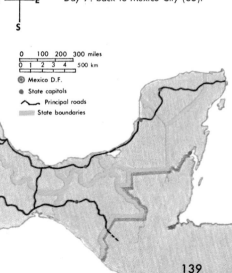

N
W — E
S

```
     0   100  200  300 miles
     0  1  2  3  4   500 km
```

◎ Mexico D.F.
● State capitols
⌒ Principal roads
▨ State boundaries

139

Seal of the United States of Mexico shows the eagle holding a snake—the omen that signified the end of the Aztec peregrinations.

THE MEXICAN GOVERNMENT has its roots in national elections held every six years. The revolutionary slogan of "effective suffrage and no reelection" is in effect. All, over 21 vote; no immediate reelection is permitted.

LEGISLATIVE branch of the government consists of a Senate and Chamber of Deputies. The Senate has sixty members; two for each state and two for the Federal District. Senators are elected for six-year terms. The Chamber of Deputies has about 180 members (one for each 200,000 people) who are elected for three-year terms. The legislature meets four months of the year (Sept.–Jan.). The rest of the time a committee deals with problems that may involve the legislature.

EXECUTIVE division of the government is headed by the President who is elected for one six-year term. Mexico has no Vice President. If the President dies while in office, action depends on how much of his term remains. If more than two years, another election is held. The President is also responsible for 15 executive departments.

JUDICIAL branch is the third arm of the federal government. At the head is the Supreme Court, backed by Circuit and District Courts. The Supreme Court has 21 members appointed by the President with the approval of the Senate. An officer, equivalent to the Attorney-General, heads the legal arm of the government.

THE SEAT of the federal government is in Mexico City. At the east side of the Plaza de la Constitucion (Zocalo) is the National Palace, office of the President. The Supreme Court building adjoins. Not far to the west, on Calle Donceles, are the Senate and Chamber of Deputies. Offices of various executive departments are scattered through the city. All of them are open to visitors. Except for the National Palace, these are not "tourist attractions."

National Palace, Zocalo, Mexico City—at sunrise.

STATE GOVERNMENTS in Mexico are patterned after the federal government. They do not have as much power as do states of the U.S. The President, for example, can remove the governor and may appoint an interim governor till the next election. State education programs are subordinate to federal programs. In other areas, results come from state and federal close cooperation.

VISITORS AND THE LAW Tourists must bear in mind that, like Mexican citizens, they are subject to Mexican law. The U.S. Embassy can offer advice and can explain procedures, but it cannot interfere.

A visitor enters Mexico on a 30-day tourist card (free) or on a 180-day card (fee $3). Neither of these permits can be renewed, and the visitor must leave before they expire. Special arrangements are possible for people who want to stay longer, especially if they are retirees, over 55, with an independent income.

An automobile may create its own legal problems. A tourist may bring in his car for a 180-day nonrenewable period. If the car is registered in another's name, a notarized statement, authorizing its use, should be in the driver's hands. It is difficult to transfer the papers for your car to another driver. If called away in an emergency, your car can be left for a reasonable time with customs officials at the airport in Mexico City.

Your home insurance policy is probably not valid abroad, and in case of accident only a Mexican insurance policy is recognized as evidence of ability to pay any claim that may be involved. Take extra care to avoid accidents. In Mexico an accident that causes bodily injury is considered a criminal offense. It is likely that the car will be impounded (and the driver, too) until responsibility is fixed. In such a situation a little Spanish, a good lawyer, and a lot of patience will help.

Library, National University

Modern rural school, Tepic

EDUCATION, Mexico's solution for major social and economic problems, gets nearly 20% of the national budget. Education means basic literacy for many; for some it opens the way to technical work or the professions; for all, it means a fuller life.

NATIONAL UNIVERSITY OF MEXICO, in University City at the Pedregal, is Mexico's symbol of higher education. Over 80,000 students (mostly part-time) are in 17 faculties and 15 research institutes. This remarkable campus was developed by a team of leading architects who blended dramatic buildings, plantings, and playing fields in a stark field of lava.

Other universities, mostly State, total 29, plus 26 other schools of higher learning and technical study. Some 200 normal schools train teachers in a six-year program. Many Mexican schools are gems of architecture (as at Monterrey). All create new opportunities. Problems remain: higher salaries for teachers and professors, more classrooms and laboratories, dormitories for students. Many universities offer summer courses for visitors, in English and in Spanish.

UNIVERSAL FREE EDUCATION is decreed for all from 6–14. To this end, over 34,000 primary schools have been built, mostly in rural areas, and over 2,000 kindergartens. Yet over 25% of the children do not attend school. The rural primary school is often a community center and the teacher's home. Each has simple but basic equipment. Textbooks are given free to students, making them also useful to parents. Adult education for basic literacy is an active program. The federal government operates all public schools, and inspects all private schools.

The success of primary education has created a need for federal, state, and private secondary schools and preparatory schools with 3-year programs. Preparatory schools prepare for college; others have terminal programs: commercial, technical, or agricultural.

Social Security Hospital

MODERN ARCHITECTURE is the trademark of modern Mexico. Its imprint is clear in the cities and even in small towns. All public buildings show the forward direction that government architects take in their work, often finishing with murals, sculpture, and paintings.

URBANIZATION, population growth, and a rising economy during the past two decades have made planning and construction an immediate need. Fortunately, young Mexican architects took the responsibility and have moved rapidly. Their aim is to combine utility, logic, aesthetics, and social values. In so doing they have adapted terrain and materials to their needs. Entire new cities have been planned and built. Master plans have been set up to rehabilitate older ones. The best examples of modern architecture will be seen in new universities, hotels, hospitals, government, and industrial buildings. See the new multifamily developments.

House of Deputies, Campeche

Museum of Anthropology

143

Latin American Tower

MEXICO CITY, the tourists' mecca, is slowly engulfing the Federal District and already spills out across the boundaries. It dominates a natural lake basin, the Valley of Mexico. Founded on the site of the Aztec capital of Tenochtitlan (pp. 88–89), the capital has inherited geographic problems. The settling sands and muds of the lake bed have not provided the best foundation on which to build a metropolis. Modern engineering has overcome most of these problems, including a new subway, and Mexico City continues to grow.

MEXICO CITY, with a population of over six million (metropolitan area), is the world's 10th largest city and truly cosmopolitan; comparable to other world capitals. One can purchase here all the crafts from distant Mexican villages. Local guide publications, many free, will give you details. Here is a summary of sights worth considering. Those in bold face type are a "must."

ARCHEOLOGY Besides the famous museum, try these, all within an hour's ride: Tenochtitlan, Aztec ruins northeast corner of Zocalo. Copilco, burials under lava, and Cuicuilco, an early "pyramid"—both in San Angel. Teotihuacan (N.W. 35 mi.), famous large pyramids. Tenayuca and St. Cecilia (N. 8 mi.), restored pyramids; and three good sites near Texcoco (N.E. 25 mi.).

MUSEUMS aplenty—most have a token admission charge. Check hours. National Museum of Anthropology, in Chapultepec Park, with outstanding exhibits; free guide service. In the new park see the Natural History Museum. Atop a hill in Chapultepec Castle is the Nat. Historical Museum. A view of the city is an added attraction. Nearby is the new Museum of the Development of Mexico. In the Pedregal, see Anahuacalli, the Diego Rivera archeology museum.

MARKETS are new, more sanitary, and not as exotic as those in villages. Jamaica is the largest produce market, best seen early in the day. Merced, Lagunilla, and San Juan are described on p. 136. You will find scores of smaller local markets once you leave the center of the city.

Museum of Modern Art

CHURCHES, modern and historical, abound. First is the Cathedral, largest in Mexico, on the Zocalo and Basilica of Guadalupe to the north. Look for new modern churches of interesting and dramatic design. Church museums are Acolman Convent (near Teotihuacan); Tepotzotlan (N.W.) and Tlalmanalco; Churubusco and El Carmen, both south in Mexico City.

ART ranges from classical to modern. Bellas Artes has shows and permanent exhibits; outstanding murals. See also the new Nat. Mus. of Modern Art in Chapultepec Park. Younger artists have outdoor shows: Sunday in Sullivan Park, Parque España, and San Angel. Murals have made Mexican art famous. See Diego Rivera's and others.

FINALLY, see the Latin American Tower, with its great view of the city. Sunday in Chapultepec Park is a Mexican family holiday. Don't forget the zoo. Also, for picnics and family outings go to the Desert of Lions (no desert, no lions), a pine woods with an old convent. Xochimilco, still worth seeing, has generally declined. A morning at University City (p. 142) shows you dramatic architecture and Mexican education.

Mexico has good foreign and local movies, including new releases. Several theaters put on plays in Spanish. You will see notices of operas, concerts, and recitals. For the serious visitor, there are programs (and courses) at the University of the Americas, Mexican-No. Amer. Cultural Inst.

Chapultepec Park   "The Angel"   Downtown Mexico

CITIES reflect what is modern in Mexico and also preserve its historic heritage. Many are large industrial, commercial, or agricultural centers. The visitor may be more interested in smaller, "unspoiled" towns. Here are some cities which, on both counts, should be considered. Visitors will find ample information on roads, food, hotels, and services. In parentheses are the direction and distance from Mexico City. See colonial monuments (p. 100).

ACAPULCO (S. 265 mi.) was once a port for Oriental trade. Now it is a delightful playground, used by Mexicans as well as visitors. Excellent swimming and fishing. Ample accommodations, plush or economical.

CUERNAVACA (S. 52 mi.) was the summer home of Aztec and Spanish rulers. See the Cathedral, Cortes Palace, and perhaps the Borda Gardens. Two pyramids can be studied, Teopanzalco near the railroad, and Xochicalco some 25 miles south. Another 20 miles gets you to the Cacahuamilpa caves.

GUADALAJARA (N.W. 370 mi.), in rich farming and cattle country, is Mexico's second largest city. Wide streets with old and new buildings; many parks. Some government buildings have famous murals. See the Cathedral, State Museum, and market. Nearby are pottery and weaving centers and Mexico's largest waterfall (30 miles).

GUANAJUATO (N.W. 220 mi.), a great mining center and a restored Colonial town with a unique subterranean road. More impressive than any one building

is the town itself, with narrow streets (one way), crowded into the narrow valley.

MERIDA (E. 955 mi.), an agricultural center for henequen, fruits, grains, and cattle. See the market, Cathedral, and State Museum. Merida is the center of a rich area of Mayan ruins (pp. 86–89) that every visitor should see.

MONTERREY (N. 610 mi.), a great industrial center with steel mills, railroad yards, and other heavy industries. See the University, Cathedral, and government buildings. A cable car runs up Saddle Mt. Some 30 miles away are the famed Garcia Caves.

OAXACA (S.E. 340 mi.), in a rich agricultural valley, is best known for its local industries and crafts (leather, cotton, steel, and black pottery). Visit the market, plaza, and museum; then head for the archeological zones of Monte Alban, Mitla, Yagul, and perhaps Zaachila (pp. 84–85). Replicas of Monte Alban jewelry are available. The great cypress, or Ahuehuete Tree (p. 24), may be seen in Tule on the way to Mitla.

Guanajuato, a modern and colonial town.

PATZCUARO (N.W. 235 mi.), on Lake Patzcuaro, is a famed center for wood, ceramics, and other crafts made by Tarascan Indians. The island of Janitzio has an Indian village and a huge statue of Morelos.

PUEBLA (E. 80 mi.) is a growing commercial center, noted for its onyx, textiles, pottery, and tiles, used lavishly on old buildings. See the Cathedral, government buildings, the Secret Convent, and the forts overlooking the city, where the French were defeated.

QUERETARO (N.W. 135 mi.), a historic town, with an impressive 18th-century aqueduct and a colorful plaza. Visit the historic sites and the shops, where opals and other stones are cut and polished.

SAN CRISTOBAL DE LAS CASAS (S.E. 735 mi.) is the market town for a number of Mayan Indian groups, whose costumes and manners intrigue visitors. Trips to the Indian villages can be arranged, though they are not anxious for visitors.

SAN LUIS POTOSI (N. 260 mi.), a mining, farming, and shipping center. Buildings of historical interest are on the plazas. There is a large market.

SAN MIGUEL DE ALLENDE (N.W. 195 mi.), an attractive Colonial city. Visit the plaza and its Gothic Parochial Church, the market and the Art Institute.

TAXCO (S. 105 mi.), a National Monument, full of almost identical silver shops. Other crafts exist, but Taxco remains the great silver center. See the Cathedral. Walk the narrow streets; visit the plaza, market, and stores.

TOLUCA (W. 40 mi.) is higher than Mexico City and capital of the state of Mexico. Noted for its Friday market and Museum of Archeology. The Calixtlahuaca Ruins are about 5 miles north.

VERACRUZ (E. 275 mi.) is a modern seaport. This is where Cortes landed in 1519; the Gringos, in 1914. Good fishing, fair swimming, and interesting trips around the bay and to nearby islands.

147

MEXICO'S PLACE among modern nations depends on its natural resources, industry, and commerce. As expected, Mexico is rich in some aspects, poor in others. On the whole, it does well. Backed by a wealth of natural resources, Mexico's gross national product rose 23% in the period 1960–65 and is moving toward $20 billion.

TRADE for Mexico runs about 4 billion dollars a year with exports somewhat exceeding imports. Nearly ¾ of the imports come from the U.S., which also gets more than ¾ of Mexico's exports. In a 30-year period, trade has increased tenfold. Internally, improved roads have brought rural areas closer.

TRANSPORTATION has made this possible. Mexico's first railroad opened in 1873. Now there are 14,000 miles of track with modern Diesel equipment. In 30 years, Mexico has built over 30,000 miles of roads; 21,000 paved. Now, four-lane limited-access highways spread from Mexico City. Buses provide transportation to remote villages.

INDUSTRY transforms raw materials into usable products. To do this, energy, machinery, and skilled workers are needed. Mexico has the energy, mainly as petroleum. Leading industries include textiles: cotton (one million tons a year), henequen, and synthetic fibers. Food processing involves sugar (one million tons a year), coffee, grains, vegetable oils, etc. In the 10-year period 1950–60, food industries doubled the number employed and tripled production. Mineral industries feature petroleum (p. 17), metals, and nonmetals. Iron production has increased most rapidly. The electrical industry produces over 12 billion kilowatt hours annually. A booming chemical industry provides paper, drugs, cement, paints, glass, and other products.

PETROLEUM Mexican oilfields cover some 3,100 sq. mi. The most important fields are in Veracruz, Tamaulipas, and San Luis Potosi, which produce about 65% of the oil. Fields in the Isthmus of Tehuantepec produce 10%.

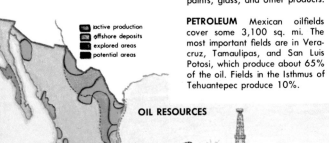

active production
offshore deposits
explored areas
potential areas

OIL RESOURCES

Petrochemical plants and refineries, at Atzcapotzalco, process Mexican petroleum into industrial and consumer products.

ENERGY RESOURCES come mainly from oil wells that produce about 120 million barrels yearly. While this is only about 5% of U.S. production, it is also only a small part of Mexico's estimated reserves of nearly 4 billion barrels. Large refineries have been built with a capacity of about half a million barrels daily.

Natural gas reserves are also great, and bottled gas is widely used as household and industrial fuel. Both petroleum and gas move through some 5,000 miles of pipeline. Petrochemical industries are developing. Mexico also has adequate deposits of soft coal. Waterpower is the last energy resource, and Mexico extracts only 1/5 of its potential 7 million kilowatts. Several new dams are under construction.

MINING, the traditional Mexican industry, is still of major importance. In addition to the mineral fuels, Mexico's mineral industries are centered mainly on metals. Mexico is still the leading producer of silver, though production is declining as is the case with gold. Zinc, copper, and lead yield enough for national needs and for export. Iron production, growing fast, is over a million tons yearly and is creating many new industries. Mexico also produces antimony, mercury, cadmium, tin, and tungsten. Coal and sulfur production is over a million tons annually. Building stones, marble, and onyx are quarried. Semiprecious stones are mined. Commercial mineral deposits occur in 22 states. Of some 20,000 mines, 400 are major producers.

149

AGRICULTURE is still the base of Mexican life, even though industry and commerce are increasing rapidly. Over half the population is engaged in agruculture and related work (as forestry). The major problems of Mexico have been agricultural, so the Revolution had land reform as a major goal. Now, 56% of the land is in over a million farms of less than five hectares (12 acres). Most of the remainder is in ejidos. Problems of credit, water, and crop yield still call for solution.

MEXICAN LAND falls into complex patterns because of soil, water, altitude, and other factors. Of some 500 million acres, only about 10% is tillable and of this about 85% requires irrigation.

In addition to the 10% tillable land, about 20% of Mexico is forest; 30% is land suited to pasture; the rest of the land is desert or submarginal.

FORESTS in Mexico were exploited even before the Conquest. Today they are in a poor state. Only about ⅓ of the trees produce timber, and except for pines, these are mainly in tropical hardwood forests. The yield is about 2 million board feet of timber yearly. Government control is now being exercised, and reforestation programs have begun.

IRRIGATION: of the tillable land, about ½ is arid and over ¼ semi-arid. And because some land is left fallow, the actual land under cultivation runs about 28 million acres at a time. These facts make irrigation essential. A nationwide program was inaugurated in 1926. Now there are over 100 irrigation districts, with dams on about 20 large rivers and many smaller ones. In some areas deep wells supply the surface water needed. In all, about 7.5 million acres are now irrigated.

SOIL CONSERVATION is a new idea in Mexico. Chemical fertilizers are new also and are still costly. Improved plants, crop rotation, contour plowing, and fallow periods help maintain the soil. There is little new land when old land is exhausted.

Red—Maize White—Wheat

Red—Beans White—Oranges

Red—Rice White—Sugar

Irrigation, near Celaya.

CROPS in Mexico are as varied as land and climate. Most important are the cereals. Corn (*maize*) is widely grown. The areas of greatest production of this and other crops are shown on the maps below. Government experts have developed many kinds of corn for Mexican soils.

Wheat is an important, and increasing, temperate crop, as bread gradually replaces the immortal *tortilla*. The warm, moist areas produce a good crop of rice. Some barley is grown in the wheat regions.

Beans of several kinds, peas, garbanzos, and lentils are also important in the Mexican diet. Beans are often grown with corn. Of the fruits, bananas are a major crop. So are citrus fruits, papayas, mangos, and mamey (pp. 50–53). More important commercially are sugarcane, coffee, and cacao, which are money crops of national importance. Tobacco is grown in amounts that meet national needs.

Finally come the important fiber crops, of which cotton is outstanding for the national textile industry and for export. Henequen is widely used for rope. Maguey fiber and jute are also produced. All are declining in importance.

CATTLE represent an important part of Mexican agriculture, though the development of high-yield stock is still new. Severe epidemics in the late 1940's crippled the cattle industry, but recovery is now complete. Mexico has over 25 million cattle; about 10 million each of goats and pigs; some 8 million sheep and at least 10 million horses, mules, and burros.

Red—Coffee
White—Cocoa

Red—Pineapple
White—Grapes

Red—Cotton

White—Henequen

151

Planting Corn—State of Mexico.

RURAL MEXICO is the hard core of the country. Here lives the *campesino*. His adobe house still has an earthen floor. His food: *tortillas, frijoles, chili,* and, occasionally, meat. His simple clothes home-made. Crude *huaraches* and a sombrero are a symbol of his status. This Mexico was a problem before the Revolution, and it still is.

RURAL MEXICO is not one place. It varies from tropical forest to worn-out, arid plateau land. Here lives the part of Mexico's population that includes nearly all the Indians (8% of total) and a good part of the mestizos (76% of population). The rural population is generally declining because the seasonal labor provides insufficient family income. Most rural land has a temperate climate that produces one crop a year. The rest of the time the land (and often the people) are idle. Small local projects bring government money to these areas. Some villages have developed crafts that provide seasonal income, depending on the market.

PART OF THE SOLUTION to rural problems has been migration to the cities. New jobs in industry help (and some industry has gone to rural areas). But new city slums have developed, which are combated by a vigorous housing program. Efforts at trade education for adults are under way. Government social service agencies have increased tremendously, but the transition from a simple, uneducated farmer to a skilled factory worker takes time. Meanwhile, help in the form of more rural schools, health centers, and technical assistance to farmers reaches even the small villages. Progress is being made —but slowly.

Harvesting sisal, Yucatan

THE EJIDO SYSTEM, useful in Colonial times, was revived in 1917, in an attempt to give every farmer some land of his own. Ejido land is communal, but the holder has a vested interest, which remains in his family after his death. Each allotment is about 10 acres—a quarter of it tillable. About 20,000 ejidos hold nearly half of Mexico's tillable land. It soon became evident that land alone was no answer. The government has pushed rural education, extended credit for tools, given technical aid, and encouraged cooperatives.

Ejidos are run democratically. And if the land is good and the leadership too, they succeed, especially if they have a cash crop, like cotton, in addition to food crops for each family. In some places poor soil, erosion, lack of water, and poor leadership have left the *campesino* almost as badly off as before.

Ejido homes—Yucatan

Butterfly net fishing on Lake Patzcuaro

FISHING is a natural occupation along Mexico's extended coastline. Much of the fishing is local, supplying family and village needs. Lack of refrigeration and good roads keeps this type of fishing on a local level. Commercial fishing, mostly in the Pacific, has developed mainly for tuna and sardines. In addition, shrimp has become an important marine product, also oysters and crabs. Over 200,000 tons of fishery products are marketed yearly.

TOURISM is the major industry of Mexico. Stimulated by better roads, larger hotels, and increased publicity, over 1.5 million visitors yearly (excluding those to border cities) spend over a billion dollars in Mexico.

TOURISM is quite new. The Pan-American Highway opened in 1934, and new roads continue to spread. Now Mexico has 45 first-class airports, and planes come by 27 routes to Mexico City. This aids tourism, since about 60% of tourists come by car and 35% by air. Most (95%, to be exact) come from the United States. In two decades tourism has increased by 700%—a tremendous growth for this "industry without chimneys."

To take care of all these visitors, over 3,000 tourist establishments have been built, of which 2,100 are hotels. These have a capacity of 165,000 people per day. The Departamento de Turismo sets standards and investigates complaints.

Fishing boat—Isla Mujeres

SCIENTIFIC NAMES

24 Monte. Bald.: *Taxodium mucronatum*
Juniper: *Juniperus deppeana*
Sacred Fir: *Abies religiosa*

25 Monte. Pine: *Pinus montezumae*
Hartweg Pine: *P. hartwegii*
Mex. White Pine: *P. ayacahuite*
Jalocote Pine: *P. patula*
Lumholtz Pine: *P. lumholtzii*
Chihuahua Pine: *P. chihuahuana*
Aztec Pine: *P. teocote*
Mex. Pinyon Pine: *P. cembroides*

26 Handflower: *Chiranthodendron pentadactylon*
Ramrod: *Chaetoptelea mexicana*
Tree Fern: *Cyathea mexicana*

27 Emory Oak: *Quercus emoryi*
Mexican Oak: *Q. mexicana*
Net-leaf: *Q. reticulata*
Wrinkle-leaf: *Q. rugosa*

28 Creosote: *Larrea divaricata*
Ocotillo: *Fouquieria splendens*
Sweet: *Acacia farnesiana*
Cat-claw: *A. greggii*

29 Mesquite: *Prosopis chilensis*
Palo: *Parkinsonia aculeata*
Des. Wil.: *Chilopsis linearis*
Lignumvitae: *Guaiacum coulteri*
Morn. Glory: *Ipomoea murucoides*

30 Nopal: *Opuntia streplacantha*
Pipestem: *O. leptocaulis*
Barrel: *Echinocactus wislizenii*
Cholla: *Opuntia imbricata*

31 1.: *Carnegiea gigantea*
2.: *Pachycereus marginatus*
3.: *Neobuxbaumis tetetzo*
4.: *Lemaireocereus weberi*
5.: *Pachycereus pringlei*
6.: *P. pecten-aboriginum*

32 Agave *atrovirens*

33 Lechuguilla: *Agave lechuguilla*
Drooping: *A. attenuata*
Henequen: *A. fourcroydes*
Mescal: *A. parryi*

34 Izote: *Yucca filifera*
Amole: *Y. elata*

35 Sotol: *Dasylirion wheeleri*
Soyata: *Beaucarnea inermis*
Nolina: *Nolina bigelovi*
Furcraea: *Furcraea longaeva*

36 Cocos *nucifera*

37 Sabal: *Sabal mexicana*
Cohune: *Orbignya cohune*
Washington: *Washingtonia filifera*
Chamaedorea: *Chamaedorea tepejilote*

38 Mahogany: *Swietenia macrophylla*
Cedro: *Cedrela mexicana*
Chicle: *Achras zapote*

39 Fig: *Ficus padifolia*
Gourd: *Crescentia cujete*
Ceiba: *Ceiba pentandra*
Lipstick: *Bixa orellana*

40 Trumpet: *Tabebuia palmeri*
Springbells: *Cybistax donnell-smithii*
Yel. Shell.: *Cochlospermum vitifolia*
Silk-cotton: *Bombax ellipticum*

41 Eucalyptus: *Eucalyptus globulus*
Peruv. Pepper tree: *Schinus molle*

42 Oleander: *Nerium oleander*
Bougainvillea: *Bougainvillea spectabilis*
Aust. Pine: *Casuarina equisetifolia*
Trop. Almond: *Terminalia catappa*

43 Frangipani: *Plumeria rubra*
Orchid: *Bauhinia variegata purpurea*
Jacaranda: *Jacaranda acutifolia*
Royal Poinciana: *Delonix regia*

44 Bamboo: *Bambusa vulgaris*
Tobacco: *Nicotina glauca*
Angel's Trumpet: *Datura arborea*
Castor Bean: *Riconus communis*
Af. Tulip: *Spathodea campanulata*

45 Prickly-poppy: *Argemone ochroleuca*
Hum.: *Beloperone californica*
Cassia: *Cassia tomentosa*
Brittlebush: *Encelia farinosa*

46 Shell: *Tigridia pavonia*
Tuberose: *Polianthes tuberosa*
Zephyr: *Zephyranthes grandifolia*
Jacobean: *Sprekelia formossissima*
Spider: *Hymenocallis sp.*

47 Dahlia: *Dahlia rosea*
Zinnia: *Zinnia elegans*
Marigolds: *Tagetes signata*
Cal. *Canendula oficinalis*
Cosmos: *Cosmos sulphureus*
Poinsettia: *Euphorbia pulcherrima*

48 *Stanhopea tigerina*
Stanhopea oculata
Laelia majans
Laelia autumnalis
Vanilla planifolia
Barqueria elegans

49 *Billbergia euphemiea*
Guzmannia lingulata
Tillandsia imperialis
Pineapple: *Ananas comosus*

50 Avocado: *Persea americana*
Mango: *Magnifera indica*
Limon: *Citrus aurantifolia*
Mamey: *Mammea americana*

Scientific Names (cont)

51 Yel. Zapote: *Lucuma salicifolia*
   Black: *Diospyros ebenaster*
   White: *Casimiroa edulis*
   Chicle: *Achras zapote*
   Marmalade: *Calocarpum sapota*
52 Papaya: *Garcia papaya*
   Soursop: *Annona muricata*
   Custard Apple: *Annona cherimola*
   Guava: *Psidium guajava* and
      P. sartorianum
   Breadfruit: *Artocarpus incisa*
   Tuna: *Opuntia tomentosa*
      O. engelmanni, etc.
53 Tamarind: *Tamarindus indica*
   Pine Nut: *Pinus cembroides*
   Coconut: *Cocos nucifera*
   Cocoa Bean: *Theobroma cacao*
   Coffee: *Coffea arabica*
   Jamaica: *Hibiscus sabdariffa*
55 Centipede: *Scolopendra heros*
   Scorpion: *Centruroides sculpturatus*
   Spider: *Lactrodectus mactans*
56 Red Snapper: *Lutjanus blackfordi*
   Sea Bass: *Stereolepis gigas*
   Snook: *Centropomus undecimalis*
57 Dolphin: *Coryphaena hippurus*
   Sailfish: *Istiophorus albicans*
   Striped Marlin: *Makaira audax*
   Tuna: *Thunnus albacares*
58 Horned Lizard: *Phrynosoma*
      platyrhinos
   Iguana: *Iguana iguana*
   Mex. Beaded Lizard: *Heloderma*
      horridum
59 Boa: *Boa constrictor*
   Fer-de-lance: *Bothrops atrox*
   Coral: *Micruroides euryxanthus*
   Racer: *Drymobius margaritiferous*
   Indigo: *Drymarchon corais*
   Garter: *Thamnopis megalops*
60 Frigate: *Fregate magnificens*
   Caracara: *Caracara cheriway*
61 Swift: *Chaetura rutila*
   Flycatcher: *Pyrocephalus rubinus*
   Mex. Motmot: *Momotus mexicanus*
   Ani: *Crotophaga sulcirostris*
   Roadrunner: *Geococcyx californianus*
62 Scarlet Macaw: *Ara macao*
   Hawk-eagle: *Spizaetus ornatus*
   Oropendula: *Gymnostinops montezuma*
   Aracari: *Pteroglossus torquatus*
   Curassow: *Crax rubra*

63 Oriole: *Icterus prosthemelas*
   Grosbeak: *Caryothraustes poliogaster*
   Jacamar: *Galbula ruficauda*
   Manakin: *Pipra mentalis*
   Wood Rail: *Aramides cajanea*
64 Thick-billed Parrot: *Rhynchopsitta*
      pachyryncha
   Flycatcher: *Ptilogonys cinereus*
   Trogon: *Trogon mexicanus*
   Solitaire: *Myadestes obscurus*
   Thrush: *Ridgwayia piniçola*
65 Grosbeak: *Hesperiphona abeillei*
   Euphonia: *Tanagra musica*
   Siskin: *Spinus notatus*
   Warbler: *Cardellina rubifrons*
   Junco: *Junco phaeonotus*
66 Kite: *Rostrhamus sociabilis*
   Oriole: *Icterus gularis*
   Flycatcher: *Muscivora tyrannus*
   Jacana: *Jacana spinosa*
   Tinamou: *Crypturellus cinnamomeus*
67 Parakeet: *Aratinga canicularis*
   Parrot: *Amazona albifrons*
   Cacique: *Cassiculus melanicterus*
   Jay: *Calocitta formosa*
   Bunting: *Passerina leclancherii*
68 Coquette: *Paphosia helenae*
   Violet-crowned: *Amazilia violiceps*
   Emerald: *Chlorostilbon canivetii*
   Berylline: *Amazilia beryllina*
   Star-throat: *Heliomaster longirostris*
   Hermit: *Phaethornis superciliosus*
69 Ringtail: *Bassariscus astutus*
   Coati: *Nasua narica*
   Kinkajou: *Potus flavus*
70 Collared: *Tayassu tajacu*
   White-lip.: *Tayassu pecari*
   Tapir: *Tapirella bairdii*
   Anteater: *Tamandua tetradactyla*
   Armadillo: *Dasypus novemicinctus*
71 Jaguar: *Felis onca*
   Jaguarundi: *F. jagouaroundi*
   Ocelot: *F. pardalis*
   Margay: *F. wiedii*
72 Howler: *Alouatta palliata*
   Spider: *Ateles geoffroyi*
   Paca: *Cuniculus paca*
   Agouti: *Dasyprocta punctata*
73 Manatee: *Trichechus manatus*
   Sea Lion: *Zalophus californicus*
   Porpoise: *Phocoena phocoena*
   Whale: *Eschrichtius gibbosus*

INDEX

157